Swift

Swift

Nigel Wood
Lecturer in English
University of Birmingham

HUMANITIES PRESS INTERNATIONAL, INC.
Atlantic Highlands, NJ

First published in 1986 in the United States of America by
HUMANITIES PRESS INTERNATIONAL, INC.,
Atlantic Highlands, NJ 07716

© Nigel Wood, 1986

Library of Congress Cataloging-in-Publication Data

Wood, Nigel,
 Reading Swift.

 (Harvester new readings)
 Bibliography: p.
 1. Swift, Jonathan, 1667–1745—Criticism and
interpretation. I. Title. II. Series.
PR3727.W66   1986   828′.509   86–412
ISBN 0–391–03416–2

PRINTED IN GREAT BRITAIN

For
Alison and Naomi

Harvester New Readings

This major new series offers a range of important new critical introductions to English writers, responsive to new bearings which have recently emerged in literary analysis. Its aim is to make more widely current and available the perspectives of contemporary literary theory, by applying these to a selection of the most widely read and studied English authors.

The range of issues covered varies with each author under survey. The series as a whole resists the adoption of general theoretical principles, in favour of the candid and original application of the critical and theoretical models found most appropriate to the survey of each individual author. The series resists the representation of any single either traditionally or radically dominant discourse, working rather with the complex of issues which emerge from a close and widely informed reading of the author in question in his or her social, political and historical context.

The perspectives offered by these lucid and accessible introductory books should be invaluable to students seeking an understanding of the full range and complexity of the concerns of key canonical writers. The major concerns of each author are critically examined and sympathetically and lucidly reassessed, providing indispensable handbooks to the work of major English authors seen from new perspectives.

'O Thou! whatever title please thine ear,
Dean, Drapier, Bickerstaff, or Gulliver!'
Pope, *The Dunciad* (1743)
Book I, ll.90–20

'Your method of concealing your self puts me in mind of
the bird I have read of in India, who hides his head in a hole,
while all his feathers and tail stick out.'
Pope, Letter to Swift, 6 January 1733/4

Contents

Prefatory Note

Swift's opinion of his future commentators was, when not dismissive, downright abusive. In the 'Digression Concerning Criticks' in A *Tale of a Tub*, they prepare 'to Read, only for an Occasion of Censure and Reproof', derive pedantic satisfaction 'from the worms, and Graves and Dust of Manuscripts', ignore the obvious from a devotion to 'Types and Figures' (the tools of the critic's trade) or set up as the '*Discoverer and Collector of Writers Faults*'. I have tried to answer most of these objections. My only certainty is that it is hardly 'the very *first* Result of the *Critick's* Mind', and was carefully nurtured by many others. My clearest debt is to former colleagues and students at Leicester and Durham. More particularly, I am immensely grateful to the Research Foundation of Durham University who had me as the University's Research Fellow of Arts whilst the book was completed, Durham's Research Fund for a trip to Dublin and Kelvin Everest who suggested the project in the first place and gave me the necessary early encouragement. Sandy Cunningham, Alan Downie and Pat Rogers read the manuscript and offered helpful advice (and correction). The faults that remain are, as one might expect, my own. Debbie Clough processed my manuscript and its several revisions both efficiently and, what is more, without objection.

I regret that David Nokes' biography of Swift was

published too late for me to incorporate his views into the main body of the text. His study is noted briefly in the Bibliography. The greatest influences on me, however, get hardly even this mention. Raman Selden often discussed with me, as supervisor and colleague, several of the book's theoretical and contemporary issues. The results of this are probably too basic and radical for individual footnotes, but the book could just not have been written at all without Alison Yarrington's help and much-needed advice.

Nigel Wood
Birmingham

Abbreviations and Principal Texts

References to Swift's works include either the volume and page number of the *Prose Works* edited by Herbert Davis or, in the case of his poetry, the page number of the *Complete Poems* edited by Pat Rogers. Fuller citations of both editions are given in the Select Bibliography.

The following abbreviations appear in the text:

[Swift] CH   *Swift: The Critical Heritage*, ed. Kathleen Williams (London, 1970).

[Defoe] CH   *Defoe: The Critical Heritage*, ed. Pat Rogers (London, 1972).

Corr.   *The Correspondence of Jonathan Swift*, 5 vols, ed. Harold Williams (Oxford, 1963–65).

SW   *Selected Writings of Daniel Defoe*, ed. James T. Boulton, (London, 1965; rep. Cambridge, 1975),

Spingarn   *Critical Essays of the Seventeenth Century*, 3 vols, ed. J. E. Spingarn (Oxford 1908; rep. 1957).

Most references are to the edition specified in the Select Bibliography. References to primary sources are either to the first edition or to the following:

Berkeley, George, *Philosophical Works including the works on vision*, introd. and notes by M. R. Ayers (London, rev. ed, 1975).

Defoe, Daniel, *Moll Flanders*, ed. Juliet Mitchell (Harmondsworth, 1978).

Robinson Crusoe, ed. J. Donald Crowley, (Oxford, 1981).

Descartes, René, *A Discourse on Method, Meditations on the First Philosophy, Principles of Philosophy*, trans. John Veitch, introd. A. D. Lindsay (London, 1912).

Erasmus, Desiderius, *In Praise of Folly*, ed. A. H. T. Levi, trans. B. Radice (Harmondsworth, 1971).

Hobbes, Thomas, *Leviathan*, ed. C. B. MacPherson (Harmondsworth, 1951).

La Rochefoucauld, François, duc de, *Maxims*, trans. L. W. Tancock (Harmondsworth, 1967).

Locke, John, *An Essay Concerning Human Understanding*, 2 vols, ed. John W. Yolton (London, 1961).

Memoirs of the Extraordinary Life, Works, and Discoveries of Martinus Scriblerus, ed. Charles Kerby-Miller (New Haven, Conn., 1950).

Milton, John, *The Poems of John Milton*, ed. John Carey and Alastair Fowler (London, 1968).

Montaigne, Michel de, *Essays*, trans. and introd. J. M. Cohen (Harmondsworth, 1958).

Pope, Alexander, *The Poems of Alexander Pope*, ed. John Butt (London, 1963).

Prior, Matthew, *The Literary Works of Matthew Prior*, 2 vols, ed. H. Bunker Wright and Monroe K. Spears (Oxford, 1959).

1

Dean

Perhaps there never was a man whose true character has been so little known, or whose conduct at all times, even from his first setting out in life, has been so misrepresented to the world, as his. . . . But the chief source of all the erroneous opinions entertained of him, arose from Swift himself. (*The Life*, 1784, Introduction)

Thomas Sheridan's verdict on Swift has been echoed by most, if not all, of his biographers. The passage of time (time enough, one would have thought, to discover revealing source material) has not helped matters. Denis Johnston in 1959 believed that any 'serious examination of the source material' would uncover 'a mass of contradictions, misdescriptions, and deliberate mendacity', where the only conclusion available was that this was 'largely deliberate'.[1] Both of Swift's most recent biographers, Irvin Ehrenpreis and J. A. Downie, have attempted investigations of scrupulous scholarship and yet, as Downie concedes in his choice of epigraph (from Hermann Hesse), one is forced to conclude, in Swift's case especially, that 'history's third dimension is always fiction' (p.

1

xvi). Whilst many writers' personalities have remained mysterious, Swift's seems unnecessarily so. On only two of his first editions, A *Proposal for Correcting, Improving, and Ascertaining the English Tongue* (1712) and the last *Drapier's Letter* (1725, although not published until 1735), was Swift's authorship actually acknowledged, and, even if such reticence provided a very thin disguise at times, the critic, as well as the biographer, must confront not only Swift's anonymity, but also his pseudonymity (as Drapier, Gulliver or Bickerstaff amongst others) that makes critical interpretation of the most basic matters, such as satiric intention or targets, so problematic.

This state of affairs poses one fundamental question about critical judgements in general, namely, what do we indicate when we 'read Swift', and to what or to whom do we refer? Until very recently the answers to such questions would probably have shown a great degree of consistency. In noting the implicit values in his writing and the rhetorical techniques he deploys to communicate them, the reader discovers patterns of thought true of both the historical 'Swift' and his work. For Irvin Ehrenpreis, for example, criticism attempted to demonstrate 'how Swift's personality could enter into his work'. The 'real person', Swift as an historical entity, sets before the reader 'visible effluences, aspects, reflections—however indirect—of an inner being that cannot be defined apart from them'.[2] For Ehrenpreis, Swift's array of personae or voices further a pre-ordained intention to which all of his rhetoric and paradoxes can be referred. Gulliver or the Teller of A *Tale of a Tub* can be summed up as 'visible effluences' of Swift's 'inner being'.

Ehrenpreis was particularly antagonistic to the American New Critics whose work on Swift stressed the techniques of which he was master rather than the 'man' himself. The novelty of their approach lay in discounting both biography and history in the interpretation of literature. New criteria that honoured subtlety and complex interrelatedness supplanted more Romantic qualities such as spontaneity or *emotional* integrity. In 'The Intentional Fallacy' (1946), W. K. Wimsatt and Monroe Beardsley proclaimed a new impersonal poetics that enshrined meaning as an effect of the words on the page rather than their writer's intention. These 'words' should claim the critic's attention rather than their writer or our own perceptions in reading them, for, in the face of linguistic and generic change, the work's meaning remained an objective element, unaltered by the process of reading which cannot alter the original design (now no longer called the 'author'). Cleanth Brooks, in his essay 'The Heresy of Paraphrase' (1947), finds the 'true' poem an experience in itself 'rather than any mere statement about experience or any mere abstraction from experience'.[3] Analysis was often limited to particular works and demonstrated how their individual parts (persona, say, or metre) fitted together. Ehrenpreis had started from 'Swift', the New Critics from his works.

The division between biographical criticism and the New Criticism is fundamental. Brooks eventually doubts that any work of literature can be paraphrased in that its true meaning is always enacted by the whole work. Ehrenpreis retains the view that, 'however indirect', the 'inner being' and its intentions can be clearly deduced. In his *Literary Meaning and Augustan Values* (1974), 'Augustan Values' are heartily endorsed as a 'real property' of Swift and his contemporaries' best work, namely 'explicit meaning, a desire for clarity' where 'they normally made explicit any doctrine they wished to indicate' (pp. 4–5). Here form and expression can achieve a direct correspondence so that statements can be clearly expressed and understood. For the New Critics the only task is to evaluate how Swift appears as a craftsman not necessarily as a moralist. Therefore, transparency of meaning even of the plainest statement, should always be judged as a *fictive* effect

3

and 'Swift' can only be deduced from the overall structure of the text rather than the individual passages that constitute it.

Both methods, however, proceed on the assumption that Swift's work is the result of more or less conscious deliberation. If we still puzzle over Gulliver's hatred of humanity or the Modest Proposer's real intentions, then that is because we have lost the key to unlock his carefully oblique meanings. Even the New Critics who often stressed the writer's impersonality kept faith with the ideal of a constancy of meaning. John Bullitt, for example, is not alone in depicting Swift's supposed objectivity as a flight from uncontrollable intensity: 'There is here a quality that transcends technical virtuosity: it is the pressure of an outraged conviction subdued and controlled by a sustained artistic intention'. This very intensity led him to exploit the available satiric tropes to such a degree that he gave them 'a permanent and challenging significance' (p. 191). In a very influential essay, Ricardo Quintana coined the term 'Situational Satire' to describe Swift's almost dramatic management of plot and varied character studies wherein no one viewpoint is ever clearly Swift, for he is deduced from the effect, not the expression. Even the dramatic 'voices' that he so adeptly ventriloquises, his personae, can be owned, eventually, by Swift as craftsman. This has been most clearly expressed by W. C. Ewald, Jr, whose recognition of Swift's 'Masks' indicates the personality which deploys them:

> In being the supposed author, the *persona* has a relation to the various attitudes and poses adopted by real authors.... The Jonathan Swift of the sermons is still Jonathan Swift when he writes indecent verses, even though his attitude is so different that he seems to be almost another person. To begin to understand the 'whole man', one must recognize all his poses. (pp. 9–10)

No matter how artifical the term 'persona' may seem, it has

roots in a very positive belief in a 'real' that underpins and regulates the surface text. For every persona one must invoke the *ethos*, or authorial presence, who has ordained its appearance.[4]

It might be remarked at this juncture: why is reliance on the notion of an artistic 'presence' or 'personality' suspect? Let me quote one conclusion from a closely argued study of Swift's rhetorical art by Martin Price; a work that, in New Critical vein, attempts to identify recurrent Swiftian themes. In concluding, Price vindicates such an analysis by defining these rhetorical devices as 'methods ... for dissociating the apparent from the real', so as to give 'the real its proper residence in, and control over, appearance' (1953, p. 111). My objection to this conclusion holds good with most strains of biographical and 'rhetorical' criticism. The grounds on which we can identify the real and the superficial in these matters are eventually *conventional* not *essential*. An 'author' can only serve a *heuristic* function in literary analysis in that the concept helps to classify certain texts with a view to providing better knowledge of them. In Swift's case especially, however, the historical entity known as 'Swift' can hardly be distinguished from the work that now bears his name. The control over appearance that Price advocates limits the possible meanings of a text according to the supposed intentions of the 'author', an individual apparently insulated from the wider social structures, linguistic possibilities or literary myths that contain the individual.

A sceptical view of this has most recently been expressed by those writers called 'Deconstructors' or 'Post-Structuralists', such as Jacques Derrida, Michel Foucault and Jacques Lacan.[5] For Derrida, in texts such as *L'Ecriture et la différance* (1967; trans. as *Writing and Difference* [Chicago, 1978] or *De la grammatologie* (1967; trans. as *Of Grammatology* [Baltimore and London, 1977], our preference for critical terms such as the 'author' or 'voice' are found to be a rhetorical means by which to manage the dangerous fertility of writing. Derrida locates such 'logocentrism' as part of a perennial western preference for *speech* (more easily identifiable as 'owned' by someone) over the bodiless residue of *writing*. 'Swift', following this train of thought, no longer exists and, indeed, even if we do have accurate biographical material to ground our hypotheses as to what his intention may have been, we would still be unaware of those unconscious yet determining factors that separate us from the early eighteenth century. The 'author-function', as Foucault calls it, brings into focus several considerations that the simpler model of the historically individual 'author' masks. Firstly, the 'author' is always 'linked to the juridical and institutional system that encompasses, determines, and articulates the universe of discourses'. These systems decide for the individual the conditions under which all expression is comprehensible and acceptable to others. Secondly, not all discourses are affected the same way 'at all times and in all types of civilization'. Thirdly, the function cannot be defined 'by the spontaneous attribution of a discourse to its producer', but rather by the complex of larger structures that contain and posit the individual's conscious freedoms as 'freedoms' indeed. Lastly, and most significantly for this reading of Swift, Foucault was careful to state that the 'author' cannot 'refer purely and simply to a real individual, since it can give rise simultaneously to several selves, to several subjects—positions that can be occupied by different classes of individuals'.[6] The coherence endorsed by the organising hand of an author is isolated as a cultural assumption and not as the natural state of affairs.

One of the results of such 'textual' readings of the author's function in critical analysis is that it frees our interpretations from an adherence to a single, fixed meaning. The very indeterminacy of written meaning fosters the proliferation of readings, and runs the risk of arriving at the paradoxes and contradictions which those following the coherence model have to ignore. This study of Swift is, therefore, an attempt to locate the functions that the first-person serves in the body of texts that bears his name. In this, I have still found the notion of the historical 'Jonathan Swift' useful even if in a diminished form. Even the New Critics had subscribed to a 'mimetic' reading, where, even though the text and its rhetoric seemed free of the author, the concept returned to authorise the particular selection of themes and patterns that most conduced to a unified work of art. In short, the text was deemed the result of an imitation of prior intentions unchanged in their expression. For the 'textual' critic, reading a work such as *Gulliver's Travels* or *A Tale of a Tub* is often an exercise in *not* looking through the writing to a writer beyond and outside it who would none the less control its metaphorical play of meanings. In Foucault's analysis, however, this verbal play need not be considered distinct from what we know of the historical institutions which gave it frames of reference, however wide. In this way are Swift's texts inescapably worldly, in that 'logocentric' pressure is not eternally the same for every text or age just as the distributions of power that influence all verbal definition cannot help but influence the possibilities in which such terms as 'novel', 'author', and 'literature' participate.

Swift's anonymity can be considered the condition of all the historical figures that serve as 'authors' in critical work. The wider historical contexts that Foucault indicates do, on the other hand, provide some notional limits to interpretation. Linguistic meaning and literary intelligibility (for example, what is 'literature' or the 'essay'?) are both part of the particular historical restraints that operate *not only* contemporaneously with the text we are reading but on ourselves too. By crossing some of the frontiers of interpretation that the 'mimetic' critics observe, we might cease to be quite so irritated by the elusiveness of Swift's meaning and start investigating its challenging multiplicity not just for the pleasure of the activity and the varied readings it promotes, but also for the awareness we gain of their particular historical context with all its incoherence and variety.

Notes

1. *In Search of Swift* (Dublin, 1959), p. 6.
2. *The Personality of Jonathan Swift* (London, 1958), p. 9; 'Personae', from *Restoration and Eighteenth-Century Literature: Essays in Honor of Alan Dugald McKillop* (Chicago, 1963), p. 31.
3. In *The Well-Wrought Urn: Studies in the Structure of Poetry* (London, 1947), p. 173.
4. The classical and rhetorical origins of this theory are discussed in Elliot, pp. 19–32; and Raman Selden, *Criticism and Objectivity* (London, 1984), pp. 124–41. The Quintana essay is entitled 'Situational Satire: A Commentary on the Method of Swift', *The University of Toronto Quarterly*, 17 (1948), 130–6.
5. 'Deconstruction' covers several critical methods that cannot always be squared one with the other. For an introductory account of its variety, see the essays in *Structuralism and Since: From Levi Strauss to Derrida*, ed. John Sturrock (Oxford, 1979), especially those on Foucault (by Hayden White), Lacan (Malcolm Bowie), and Derrida (Jonathan Culler). For the opposition between Derrida and Foucault, see Edward Said's account, pp. 178–225.
6. From 'What is an Author?', in *Textual Strategies: Perspectives in Post-Structuralist Criticism*, ed. J. V. Harari (Ithaca, N.Y., 1979), p. 153.

2

Bickerstaff

Isaac Bickerstaff was born in January 1708, when Swift had him produce his *Predictions for the Year 1708*, 'written to prevent the People of *England* from being further imposed on by vulgar Almanack-makers'. Bickerstaff's own astrology is to be an object lesson to 'those gross Imposters, who have set up to be the Artists' of predicting, so that the 'Art' itself might be rescued from disgrace. The effect of the pamphlet, however, is no 'large and rational Defence of this Art', an essay Bickerstaff promises the patient reader in the near future, but rather its exposure as an art of deception and sensationalist journalism. Swift's Bickerstaff innocently quotes 'several learned Men' who have found astrology a 'Cheat' and who hold it 'absurd and ridiculous' that 'the Stars can have any Influence at all upon human Actions, Thoughts, or Inclinations'. Almanacs provide, in their view, impertinent nonsense 'which they offer to the World as genuine from the Planets; although they descend from no greater a Height than their own Brains' (II: 141-2). Bickerstaff's bumptious confidence in his power to overcome such objections is a sure sign that the 'learned men' may indeed be right.

Swift's pretext for the attack was what he felt to be the insidious popularity in London of this occult inspiration, and its power to advise the curious in their dilemmas to the exclusion of rational or moral premises of conduct. Ethical choice no longer required strength of faith or character, for its systematising first princples were universally applicable. If all human behaviour was determined by the stars and moon, the strenuous attempt to adapt one's education and appreciation of the humane arts for spiritual benefit was fruitless. Meanwhile, booksellers and the fake prophets they publicised grew rich. The most notable of the latter, John Partridge, Swift singled out for particular mischief, for the first prediction was that he would 'infallibly die upon the 29th of *March* next, about eleven at Night of a raging Fever'. He was, therefore advised to 'settle his Affairs in Time'. *The Accomplishment of the first of Mr. Bickerstaff's Predictions* (1708) duly reported his passing with all the circumstantial and elegiac gravity of an eye-witness report. Partridge apparently confessed on his death-bed to the deceits of astrology and to his being a Nonconformist in religion, and then died a plausible four hours earlier than in Bickerstaff's prediction.

Despite protesting his existence in the next year's almanac, the *Merlinus Liberatus* for 1709, Partridge's textual credibility had been savagely mauled. A whole sub-culture of non-Swiftian but still Bickerstaffian predictions continued to parody Partridge's rhetorical authority until well after his physical death in 1715. Try as he might to dub himself 'A Lover of Truth' in the *Merlinus* for 1709 and assert that he was '(excepting my Age) as well as ever I was in my Life; as I was also at that 29th of *March*' (naturally enough), he could not recover. Partridge had become a 'Partridge'; his assertion of life, if not tautologous, demonstrated self-defeating naivety not the necessary oracular perception. Indeed, Bickerstaff had an extension of life when Richard Steele assumed the name for the pseudonymous author–editor of *The Tatler* which appeared in April 1709.

Although a local reference, Swift's ridicule of Partridge exposed him more as a symptom than a first cause of social irresponsibility. As such Partridge was as much a symbol as comic butt. In his *Elegy on the Supposed Death of Mr. Partridge, the Almanac Maker* (1708) Swift draws several elaborate and forceful parallels between making almanacs and mending shoes, Partridge's previous occupation.

> A scrap of parchment hung by geometry
> (A great refinement in barometry)
> Can like the stars foretell the weather;
> And what is parchment else but leather?
> Which an astrologer might use,
> Either for almanacs or shoes.
>
> (ll.41–6)

Thus may an art with pretensions to mystical enlightenment be conflated with one motivated by the most basic concerns of commercial expediency and dry feet. Deep within his cobbler's 'leathern cell', mending desperately to meet customers' needs for the morning, Partridge could 'in his fancy fly as far,/To peep upon a twinkling star' (ll.54–6, p. 94). Here we see a recasting of the charge that astrology was merely an irrational fixation, a displacement into written form of phantoms plucked from no greater height than the writer's own brain, and which were sublimated by either an inability to cope with sordid reality or an intense desire to escape from it by a plausible confidence trick. Madness, manifested here by astrology, is, however, transformed into criminality by the public's dangerous credulity. Poor Partridge is scarcely allowed even the guile of a criminal huckster, for he cannot help himself; his customers should know better, and when, led by a residual yearning for a quick

11

fortune, they flock to his grave and survey the 'earth which bears his body's print', (1. 103) it will inform them as well 'In physic, stolen goods, or love,/As he himself could, when above' (ll.107–8, p. 96). The inert physical *imprint* of his carcase produces as much substance or revelation as the *print* of a *Merlinus Liberatus*. Swift associates several vices with the example of both Partridge and Bickerstaff. Such hack journalism subverts literary ideals by its materialistic motivation, but the *Elegy*'s midnight portrait depicts a figure spiritually benighted as well, stealing from his 'private cell by night' not on the wings of poetry or religious contemplation but, bat-like, to obey the blind instinct of flying about the candle-light (ll.50–2, p. 94). The poem bristles with puns and innuendoes that confront abstract qualities by the possibility of their material significance. The 'print' that is the form in which predictions appear is identical with purely bodily pressure; inner spiritual light when viewed commonsensically is merely candle-light which evinces blind instincts, not universal truths. The Soul cannot escape the Body. Milton's *Il Penseroso* (1631) has its contemplative narrator star-gazing, trying to trace 'The immortal mind that hath forsook/Her mansion in this fleshly nook:' (ll.91–2, p. 143). Swift's parody regards this severance of spirit from body as fatal, at the same time as demonstrating the madness of confusing one with the other. Whereas Milton's Contemplator envisaged enjoying a 'prophetic strain' where, with the help of devotional anthems, the self might be dissolved into 'ecstasies', and 'all heaven' be brought into view (ll.155–74, p. 146), Partridge can only expect his light to be extinguished by the 'pissing' of 'roguish boys in stormy nights' (ll.75–6, p. 95).

Partridge is explicitly associated with the anarchic desperation and poverty, both literary and financial, of Grub Street hacks. When the poem was reprinted in the 1711 *Miscellanies*, its title had become *A Grubstreet Elegy* .... The original version emphasised Partridge's lineage in lines subsequently omitted:

> Consider where the moon and stars
> Have their devoutest worshippers.
> Astrologers and lunatics
> Have in More Fields their stations fix, ...
> (quoted p. 629)

As Pat Rogers points out, Grub Street, in Moorfields, 'was not a state of mind but an actuality. By a species of metonymy, the literal environment of the street came to colour the figurative sense of the term' (1972, pp. 44–5). As in Pope's *Dunciad* (1728; rev. 1743), Swift's Grubean muse inspires in close proximity to Bedlam or Bethlem Hospital, a madhouse. Bad art seemed allied to madness in more than topography.

In *A Tale of a Tub* and *A Discourse Concerning the Mechanical Operation of the Spirit* (both 1704), the mechanistic imposition of schemes and universal designs leads to fragmentation and formlessness. The contemplative man, alone in his Platonist watchtower, cannot descend and hope to have his transcendental truths accompany him. When Gulliver returns from the Houynhynms his audience is composed either of his own horses or ourselves his readers, who are all too likely to reject him for either his pride or his misanthropy. As Denis Donoghue notes, Swift is concerned with problems that should be commonly apprehensible as 'value resides in time and place, in the social world, if it resides anywhere' (p. 88). The Modern Hack of *A Tale* sets out to 'proceed in a manner, that should be altogether new', proud that 'the Authors Wit' is 'entirely his own' and that 'he has not borrowed one single Hint from any Writer in the World' (I: 1,6). The result is original but incomprehensible. The Mechanic of the Spirit desires to elevate the '*Soul or its Faculties above Matter*' by dint of religious Enthusiasm. Consequently, his brain resembles merely 'a Crowd of little

13

Animals, but with Teeth and Claws extremely Sharp' and his motivation is merely intense sexual frustration (I: 174, 181). Such ideals are portrayed as no more than physical responses. Extreme originality is a form of religious Nonconformity and modern literary pride. Whilst not quite believing in rationally derived systems, Swift could hardly embrace their opposite, mere sensual anarchy. In his earliest writings the search for a sociable and humane compromise was mapped by two ideologies in particular: Anglicanism and a classical (or Ancient) literary taste. These provide both his conceptual boundaries and his allusive terrain.

Swift's Anglicanism

In the Merlinus for both 1706 and 1707, Partridge indulges in some virulent criticism of 'Rome's little Hobby-Horse', the High Church clergy (II: x–xii). Consequently, Bickerstaff has him die a Nonconformist with a 'fanatick Preacher' as 'spiritual Guide' (II: 155). His wish to pre-ordain the future in his predictions uncovers as much presumption to inner revelation as his religious enthusiasm, for he cannot command time or, indeed hope to reduce it to a system of probabilities. Reality is not negotiable. The Aeolists of A Tale believe themselves inspired and yet 'affirm the Gift of BELCHING, to be the noblest Act of a Rational Creature' (I: 96). Intense spiritual aspirations highlight the carnal limitations of mankind. Extremes presuppose one another. Jack and Peter may represent in A Tale's religious allegory the utter extremes of Dissenter and Papist, yet, in Swift's terms, they are kin for

> the Phrenzy and the Spleen of both having the same Foundation, we may look upon them as two Pair of Compasses, equally extended, and the fixed Foot of each, remaining in the same

14

Center; which, tho' moving contrary Ways at first, will be sure to
encounter somewhere or other in the Circumference. (I: 127)

Moderation opposes both Catholicism and Nonconformity.

The compass image is a method by which Swift can balance
potentially anarchic extremes. Three years earlier he had used
it to illustrate true anarchy in A *Discourse of the Contests and
Dissentions Between the Nobles and Commons in Athens and
Rome*, his first political essay, which drew an extended
analogy between classical politics and recent British history.
Swift's political programme is committed to a framework
wherein the monarchy, government and Commons exist
peaceably by an equitable distribution of power.[1] Chaos is
come again when one estate gains a preponderance of power
such as he feared might be the present case with the
Commons for 'to fix one foot of their Compass wherever
they think fit, and extend the other to such terrible Lengths,
without describing any Circumference at all; is to leave us,
and themselves, in a very uncertain State'. The freedom to
wield power or hold an opinion wherever we think fit
involves us inevitably in the terrible uncertainty of a limitless
void, without definition or true value. 'How far must we
proceed, or where shall we stop? *The Raging of the Sea* and *the
Madness of the People*, are put together in Holy Writ; and it is
God, alone, who can say to either, *Hitherto shalt thou pass, and
no farther*' (I: 231). The Deity, in such cases, functions almost
as an eleventh-hour troubleshooter, arbitrating providentially
between individual appetites. Some all-engrossing framework
is therefore necessary not just to ensure order but, further, to
provide any value and power of definition, both verbal and
intellectual.

Swift's earliest work explores aesthetically, morally and
politically the possibilities of defining such moderation
without systematising its effects and properties or indulging
in solipsistic 'Free-Thinking'.[2] Such balance is apprehended

15

in *The Contests and Dissentions* by two metaphors, that of the body politic as a human body or that of the required power-sharing as a hand holding a balance or pair of scales. The first words of the essay affirm that 'there is an absolute unlimited Power, which naturally and originally seems to be placed in the whole Body, wherever the executive Part of it lies' in either the head, heart or hand (I: 195). The balance of power is imaged as a metaphorical balance 'held by a third hand, who is to deal the remaining Power with the utmost Exactness into each Scale'. Whenever this tenuous equipoise is disturbed 'whether by the Negligence, Folly, or Weakness of the Hand that held it, or by mighty Weights fallen into either Scale' (I: 197), tyranny results. Changes may occur but the 'Form' must still 'continue, and the Ballance be held', and, to aid this, 'large Intervals of Time must pass between every such Innovation enough to melt down, and make it of a Piece with the Constitution' (I: 202). The forms of life are so naturally regulated that systems cannot help us apprehend them. Furthermore, to probe and pry in matters of belief is the hallmark of the anti-traditional Deist and rationalist Free-Thinker, who examine God's perfection and His ineffable mysteries by the light of their own reason and who, therefore, deny the power of divine revelation. This doctrine is clearly adumbrated in his sermon 'On The Trinity', where faith is highlighted as the cornerstone of religious life, and as far more reliable than one's own capacity for reason, for '*Reason* itself is true and just, but the *Reason* of every particular Man is weak and wavering, perpetually swayed and turned by his Interests, his Passions, and his Vices' (IX: 166). The truth is with God and not Man. Swift is perpetually attempting to defend his religion by identifying its traditional mainstream. Schisms merely introduce tempting meanders. Philip Harth has shown how Swift pursued a middle course between Deists and enthusiastic Fideists who, as did the Puritans of the previous century, denied all learning or rationality. Taking

Richard Hooker's seminal *Of the Laws of Ecclesiastical Polity* (1594-7) as their authority, these rational Anglicans regarded their religion as maintaining national stability and, through that, the transindividual yardstick of a rational ideal freed from Interests, Passions and Vices.

Where then could Swift be sure that he had identified this pattern of humble rationality? This query is especially pressing given the excessive partisan strife that confronted the most minor cleric. A credo asserted merely by a translucent vocabulary and untrammelled syntax was desirable yet unattainable, for words and their power to define reality formed a particularly fraught arena for the struggles between High and Low Church, Tory and Whig, or Anglican and extremist. The enemy is elusive.

Whilst preaching moderation as one of the most constant *Sentiments of a Church of England Man, with Respect to Religion and Government* (1708), Swift advises a withdrawal from the highly charged political sphere, for fear of aiding a temporarily powerful interest to assimilate Anglicanism, first principles and all. Liberty of conscience for the Dutch, for example, had created a 'Commonwealth, founded on a sudden, by a desperate Attempt in a desperate Condition, not formed or digested into a regular System, by mature Thought and Reason, but huddled up under the Pressure of sudden Exigences' (II: 7). Consequently, election is far less satisfactory than an hereditary succession (II: 18). Furthermore, so rapid were recent changes that Swift felt that the prevailing 'Spirit of Faction' could have the power to mingle with 'the Mass of the People' and perhaps alter their 'Nature and Manners, and the very Genius of the Nation'. It could gain a foothold by travestying the truly moral vocabulary which included 'Virtue, Honour, Piety, Wit, good Sense, or Learning'. Instead, the 'modern Question is only, Whether he be a *Whig* or a *Tory*; under which Terms all good and ill Qualities are included' (II: 24). The Toleration Act (1689) had

17

been a sign of the times, for the Glorious Revolution, in underpinning political stability in its toleration of Protestant Dissent, effectively terminated the life of a single, seamless state Church. Dissenting academies could now openly offer an alternative curriculum to the less practical Oxbridge immersion in verbal and discursive skills. This new Anglicanism even allowed Presbyterian Members of Parliament when the Act of Union with Scotland was passed in 1707. Latitudinarian tolerance, according to Margaret Jacob, had 'devised a natural religion comprehensive enough to provide doctrinal differences and so broad in its application as to include behaviour once labelled simply as unchristian' (p. 49). Anglicanism was not what it was.

Swift himself had to make his way in a world that had rapidly become secularised and where the Church's highest court, Convocation, could not even suppress such obviously rationalist tracts as John Locke's *The Reasonableness of Christianity* (1695) or John Toland's *Christianity not Mysterious* (1696). Swift, ordained priest in Ireland in 1695, encountered the effects of ecclesiastical decline (especially in the Church of Ireland) at first-hand. His living at Kilroot gave him no parish church of his own and, thanks to its predominantly Presbyterian population, very small congregations. The rash of doctrinal pamphlets in 1708–9 was the fruit of his mission to England from 1707 to solicit a gift of clerical revenue, the First Fruits and Twentieth Parts (known as Queen Anne's Bounty), for the Irish clergy. Although notionally a Whig at this date and most certainly paying court to the Junto Whigs he had known during his last visit (1703–4), this period marks a period of shifting allegiances not only on Swift's part, but also within the older Whig ranks too. As J. A Downie points out, 'Swift had viewed the Revolution Settlement as a return to a situation which had obtained in the past [before the growing tyranny of James II]: the Modern Whigs increasingly regarded the events of 1688 as the foundation of a new political system' (p. 82). By 1709, Swift found Whig support for the practice of Occasional Conformity (Dissenters receiving Anglican communion just once a year to qualify for public office) inexcusable. In 1710, his new hopes for public preferment rested on the new Tory ministry and Robert Harley in particular, who allowed the remittance of the First Fruits to proceed. Swift might have changed party, but he had not altered his moral bearings. What had altered, according to to Swift, were the currents of fashion. The most immediate goal, therefore, was to try to separate what was *essentially* true from its *nominal* appearance in the world.

The urgency of this analysis for Swift was fostered by his recognition, in his *Argument Against Abolishing Christianity* (1708), that just as 'the Genius of a Nation is liable to alter in half an Age', so its language would too. What once might have been a living relationship between the word and the aspect of reality it defined could quickly die. Even the 'System of the Gospel' could become 'generally antiquated and exploded' (II: 27). This fear was no doubt reinforced by Swift's sojourn at Moor Park with his patron, Sir William Temple (1689–90, 1691–94, 1696–99).[3] Temple's perspective on modern eloquence and manners was a tragic one. In his essay *On Ancient and Modern Learning* (1690) the root problem was linguistic:

> If our Wit and Eloquence, our knowledge or Inventions would deserve it, yet our Languages would not; there is no hope of their lasting long, nor of anything in them; they change every Hundred Years so as to be hardly known for the same, ... so as they can no more last like the Ancients, than excellent Carvings in Wood like those in Marble or Brass. (Springarn, III: 63)

For Swift, it was the very condition of a culture that it tended to decay. Bickerstaff's 'murder' of Partridge was a simple affair in that almanac-makers were nominal literary personalities in the first place.

19

What fascinated Swift about Bickerstaff's success was that Partridge's cunning could be used against him; he who lived by a reader's credulity could die by it, for the Man of Print could be executed in Print. The joke of A *Vindication of Isaac Bickerstaff, Esq.* (1709) was that it dared Partridge to prove 'Merlin' had a reality outside his own bad art, in short, to prove his *ethos*. The yardstick for this is artistic potency, not bodily presence. Bickerstaff's first proof that Partridge is no more rests with how he is read:

> Above a Thousand Gentlemen having bought his Almanacks for this Year, merely to find what he said against me; at every Line they read, they would lift up their Eyes, and cry out, betwixt Rage and Laughter, *They were sure no Man alive ever writ such dammed Stuff as this.* Neither did I ever hear that Opinion disputed ...

Partridge, therefore, either had to proclaim his death in art or in life. The doubt rests as to just where his 'life' could be found: 'But know, if an *uninformed* Carcass walks still about, and is pleased to call it self *Partridge*; Mr. *Bickerstaff* does not think himself any way answerable for that' (II: 162). In literature, 'life' is ensured in rhetorical terms which almanac-makers cannot master. Their names such as Merlin, Gadbury or Dove can be passed on from age to age without any perceptible change in form or content: 'Now the natural Reason of this I take to be, that whereas it is the Privilege of other Authors, *to live after their Deaths*; Almanack-makers are alone excluded; because their Dissertations treating only upon the Minutes as they pass, become useless as those go off'; therefore, their *ethos*-free forms of writing are allowed to continue, precisely *because* they establish only the most nominal relationship with their age.

On the other hand, Partridge's ephemerality was worrying too. If a writer's fate is in the hands of his consumers, what ensures the continuance of great art? Indeed, a whole

Christian culture could succumb to transient market forces as well.

A Nominal Vocabulary and An Argument Against Abolishing Christianity

The first words of An Argument portray a persona acutely conscious of public opinion: 'I am very sensible what a Weakness and Presumption it is, to reason against the general Humour and Disposition of the World.' The Arguer is only too aware that this would be 'a manifest Breach of the Fundamental Law, that makes this Majority of Opinion the Voice of God' (II: 26). For Swift, the Hydra-headed mob could not be divine. In The Contests and Dissentions Swift had shown a great faith that 'common Sense and plain Reason', as long as people are 'disengaged from acquired Opinions', would eventually prevail. Consequently, 'the Species of Folly and Vice ... so different in every Individual' cannot win general assent for long (I: 232). Individual variety of opinion needs to be corrected. Under the cloak of nominal social 'virtues' lie the most private vices; each person is capable of his own perversity, so there must be incentives for keeping it securely within the private domain. A Project for the Advancement of Religion, and the Reformation of Manners (1709), in outlining moral reformation inspired by the example of Queen Anne, is most concerned with social mores, the 'Manners' of her subjects, rather than their existential anxieties. If religious rectitude were known to be a necessary 'Step to Favour', then many more would profess it. This seems sufficient, for the 'proudest Man' would 'personate Humility' and the laziest would be 'sedulous and active': 'How ready therefore would most Men be to step into the Paths of Virtue and Piety, if they infallibly led to Favour and Fortune?' (II: 50). In Gulliver's Travels the King of

21

Brobdingnag sees 'no Reason, why those who entertain Opinions prejudicial to the Publick, should be obliged to change, or should not be obliged to conceal them ... for, a Man may be allowed to keep Poisons in his Closet, but not to vend them about as Cordials' (XI: 131). Even though this is nominal Christianity, it will suffice, for the 'Disposition of the World', for want of a more radical spirituality, is powerful enough.

In trying to create a coherent 'Jonathan Swift' out of these early texts, however, we might ignore two contradictions, or at least contrary sentiments. First, in acknowledging the power of public credos or manifestos, it would still seem debatable whether Swift always *endorsed* this state of affairs. Private poisons were poisons still. By addressing his remedies purely to the surface of social intercourse, he seems to be aiming far short of a universal solution. The majority opinion is not the 'Voice of God'; why then minister only to public behaviour? Should hypocrisy be an adequate substitute for private reformation? Or is this a bitter compromise, fallen mankind being what it is, that testifies to Swift's cynical realism? Partridge formed a threat because his proselytising was successful, an example of Swift's fear in *The Examiner* no. 14 (9 November 1710), that there was a 'natural Disposition in many Men to *Lye*, and in Multitudes to *Believe*.' Consequently, he feels himself 'perplexed what to do with that Maxim, ... That *Truth will at last prevail*' (III: 12).

Secondly, the clear communication of ideas seems constantly bedevilled by language's endless adaptability to totally subjective, and often fraudulent, aims. The terms Tory and Whig, for example, only have a clear reference in very particularised circumstances; otherwise, they quickly become party cant, playing on people's willing credulity. The previous government of Junto Whigs Swift was ready to disown in 1710 for its blinding of 'Understandings' wherein enemies and friends had become indistinguishable (III: 12). The

Revolution had been less than glorious for Swift. Arbitrary monarchical tyranny had been averted, but the cost to ethical judgement had been great: 'I would be glad to ask a Question about *two Great Men* of the late Ministry, how they came to be *Whigs?* And by what figure of Speech, half a dozen others, lately put into great Employments, can be called *Tories?*' If one suited 'the Definition to the Persons', the direct opposite situation now held to what was understood 'at the Time of the Revolution' (III: 15). Language's figurative power seemed no privilege at all. On the contrary, Swift is flung back onto a most materialistic linguistic philosophy, where words are constantly called to account by a 'reality' deduced from 'the Persons' themselves: a physical substance free of verbal shadows. How, therefore, can one hope to reason with the 'Disposition of the World', if not by a forensic vocabulary, cleared of distracting associations and false sentiments? Swift, however, wilfully persists in ventriloquising an array of personae, and, as both David Nokes and Frederik N. Smith point out, he constantly exploits verbal ambiguities, puns and innuendoes throughout his writing career.[4]

A profile of the early Swift's ethical perspectives contains, therefore, quite a few inconsistencies. His occasional endorsement of purely nominal morality for the good of society can be read as a restatement of Bernard de Mandeville's tolerance of private vices for their creation of public benefits. In *The Grumbling Hive, or Knaves Turned Honest* (1705), enlarged as *The Fable of the Bees* (1714–29), the bee community's prosperity crumbles with its moral reformation. Before, 'every Part was full of Vice,/Yet the whole Mass a Paradice' (ll.155–6). Their 'Crimes conspired to make 'em Great' (1. 162), for Luxury and Pride were great employers of those who would otherwise go hungry.

Satisfied Virtue feels, as a result, no incentive to achieve the rewards of industry. Martin Price believes that *An Argument against Abolishing Christianity* portrays a man 'like

23

the artful managers of *The Fable of the Bees*, ... cool in his detachment and able to see what those enmeshed in ideology are too preoccupied to notice' (1964, p. 191). Mandeville's work is, on the contrary, highly ideological in its endorsement of a *laissez-faire* political structure freed from ethical considerations.[5] Swift's Arguer demonstrates the same insouciance but with radical differences in effect.

Swift's desire for a language insulated from a drift towards nominalism is really another facet of this same concern for a close relationship between both a private morality and its public profession, and the world and the language used to represent it. One of the most pervasive observations of his *Project for the Advancement of Religion* is that 'there must always of Necessity be some Corruptions', but in the well-instituted state such failings will provoke the 'executive Power' to minimise them 'by *reducing Things* ... to their *first Principles*' (II: 63). The same management is expected in literary matters. In *The Sentiments* the 'unlimited Liberty' to publish irreligious thoughts is a 'Scandal' (II: 10), and the *Project* becomes nostalgic when dwelling on 'the Office of Censors antiently in *Rome*' (II: 49). One of the few tracts to bear Swift's name is his *Proposal for Correcting, Improving and Ascertaining the English Tongue* (1712) in which he calls for an Academy charged with the responsibility of '*Ascertaining* and *Fixing* our language for ever, after such alterations are made in it as shall be thought requisite.' A systematic, and therefore static language, even if not 'wholly perfect', is preferable to one 'perpetually changing' (IV: 14). Language, because it responds to temporal changes, is, to Swift, therefore undergoing continual corruption. In *Tatler* no. 230 (28 September 1710), the productions of Grub Street, once identifiable by sheepskin binding 'with suitable Print and Paper; ... and taken off wholly by common Tradesmen, or Country Pedlars', can be seen 'gilt, and in Royal Paper of five or six Hundred Pages, and rated accordingly' by 'Persons of

Quality' (II: 174). The natural relationship between inner and outer has been destroyed. In both the *Proposal* and *Tatler* no. 230, the answer to this debasement of polite behaviour in all its forms, social, ethical and literary, is a simplicity which withstands transient modes and garish ornamentation, and which ensures continuity amidst change. This quality stands forth as 'the best and truest Ornament of most Things in human life, which the politer Ages always aimed at in their Building and Dress, ... as well as their Productions of Wit.' In contrast appears the 'new affected Modes of Speech' which 'are the first perishing Parts in any Language' (II: 177). In linguistic affairs 'simplicity' is part of this same reduction to '*first principles*' that, in government, should ensure a mitigation of corrupt practices.

There is yet further uncertainty about contemporary language: that its survival might camouflage the death of the reality it once helped delineate. The Arguer laments the stubborness of certain purely nominal words, perhaps the result of 'grievous Prejudices of Education'. Virtue and honour are examples of such survivals. Obviously, Swift's moral thesis is that these qualities exist because they conform to some deep-seated human need. His realistic fear, however, could be that such deep structures themselves might steal away, unannounced by any public means. The Arguer observes 'how difficult it is to get rid of a Phrase, which the World is once grown fond of, although the Occasion that first produced it, be entirely taken away.' In his view such ill-founded longevity might even have been misconceived in the first place. For instance, 'if a Man had but an ill-favoured Nose', he claims that as the only origin of moral distinctions: 'From this Fountain are said to be derived all our foolish Notions of Justice, Piety, Love of our Country; all our Opinions of God, or a future State, Heaven, Hell, and the like' (II: 33). Caught up in his purely corporal 'imagination', the Arguer cannot understand any innate idea at all. Swift's

25

simplicity wages a sort of trench warfare with this materialism.

This conflict took place within an arena largely formed by John Locke whose *Essay Concerning Human Understanding* (1690) had attacked the concept of any ideal conception free of an experiential cause. Thomas Hobbes' *Leviathan* (1651) had treated mankind and its universe as mechanical matter alone. As a result, the attributes of 'True' and 'False' he considered 'of Speech, not of Things. And where Speech is not, there is neither *Truth* nor *Falshood*' (Part I, Ch. 4, p. 105). With Locke however, 'Speech' was considered as a direct attribute of reality, the signified directly determining the terms of its signifier. In this sense, language could be 'the great bond that holds Society together' (III, xi, 1, vol. 2, p. 106), in that it signifies those areas of common agreement, that is, common experience. Lack of 'distinct ideas' can thus lead to ambiguity, an unfruitful state of being (III, x, 26, 29, vol. 2, pp. 103–4). In the fourth edition of the *Essay* (1700), Locke added another possible cause of ambiguity: an association of ideas that, not based on nature, might overwhelm consensual unities. This 'connexion of *ideas*' is formed 'wholly owing to chance or custom: *ideas*, that in themselves are not at all of kin, come to be so united in some men's minds that it is very hard to separate them, they always keep in company' (II, xxxiii, 5, vol. 1, p. 336). It is therefore eminently possible that Swift's 'Simplicity' is a bulwark against a private irrationalism, prey to unfortunate experiences. Hence there arose a desire to find a style and language freed from material causes.

Swift's desire to limit change in the years 1710–14 can also be explained by the fact that he was then enjoying the sunshine of the Tory government's favour, Robert Harley's in particular. The *Proposal* is in the form of a letter to Harley, newly created the Earl of Oxford, and it attracted at least two virulent Whig rejoinders: John Oldmixon's *Reflections on Dr.*

Swift's letter to the Earl of Oxford and *The British Academy* of composite (Whig) authorship (both 1712). Oldmixon considered it strange of Swift to regard panegyric 'the most *barren of all Subjects'* (p. 13), when his *Proposal* seemed so determined to earn the Earl's favour. Swift's public partisanship does, indeed, seem a little compromised if we consider two works, both unpublished in his lifetime: *A Modest Defence of Punning* (1716) and *A Discourse to Prove the Antiquity of the English Tongue* (c. 1727). *A Modest Defence* (IV: 205–10) is a virtuoso display of punning that celebrates the freedom of language to escape the domination of cognition and the plain style. *A Discourse* attempts to provide an argument that Hebrew, Greek and Latin were derived from English. It is a piece of Modern presumption dedicated to one of the comic butts of *The Battel of the Books*: Dr Richard Bentley. Through a series of philological pedantries we are led to the conclusion that 'the Greeks, the Romans, and the Jews, spoke the language we now do in England' (IV: 239). Swift's sentiments here seem at odds with the Proposer of improvements in 'the English Tongue'. His Academy would seek to provide a situation where all past writings were equally accessible to contemporary comprehension. In so doing he unwittingly allied himself with linguistic materialists such as Bishop John Wilkins in his *Essay Towards a Real Character and a Philosophical Language* (1668) and the Discourser of 1727.[6] David Nokes finds this irony unresolved throughout Swift's writing career:

> As a Christian humanist, Swift wished to leave men free to find their own path to salvation through this world of challenging moral ambiguities where things are often not what they seem. As a satirist he strews his writings with specious analogies, logical culs-de-sac, rhetorical booby-traps to expose the unwary. Yet all this disruptive energy goes underground when he poses as a public figure of church and state. (Probyn, 1978a, p. 49)

For all his apparent eagerness in supplying a model of linguistic transparency the most flagrant example of an irreconcilable split between the private and public, the inner and outer man, could be Swift himself.

This is, however, far from a blemish. The *Argument Against Abolishing Christianity* provides Job's comfort for the established Church, in that the Arguer is at pains to defend only nominal religious observances, true Christianity 'having been for some Time wholly laid aside by general Consent, as utterly inconsistent with our present Schemes of Wealth and Power' (II: 28). This Mandevillian cynicism is presumably set up only to be knocked down. The 'Majority of Opinion' is surely not 'the Voice of God', especially as it 'is liable to alter in half an Age'. On the other hand, '*real* Christianity', if suddenly introduced, has as anarchic an effect, for, whilst acting directly on personal belief and activity, it could still appear 'a wild Project', and

> dig up Foundations; . . . destroy at one Blow *all* the Wit, and *half* the Learning of the Kingdom; . . . break the entire Frame and Constitution of Things; . . . ruin Trade, extinguish Arts and Sciences with the Professors of them; in short, . . . turn our Courts, Exchanges and Shops into desarts. (II: 27)

If this is so, is not the remedy worse than the disease? When arguing for the prevention of new sects in *The Sentiments*, Swift illustrated their contaminating effects by the image of the man 'who should pull down and change the Ornaments of his House, in Compliance to every one who was disposed to find fault as he passed by' (II: 5). In time this might destroy the whole building. The radical step of reintroducing real Christianity accomplishes the same demolition.

The Arguer is therefore caught within an ideology that, as is the case with all ideologies, achieves a specious coherence, for it would seem that its known evils are preferable to the uncharted possibilities of revolutionary change. Nominal

Christianity is actually a force for social cohesion. Gulliver would find such hypocrisy unthinkable after the instinctive morality of the Houyhnhnms but they were not human. Such a dichotomy has become a lively critical problem. Irvin Ehrenpreis finds the talent for impersonation a basic Swiftian quality. In the *Argument*, and *A Modest Proposal* (1729), there is evident self-parody, 'in which the hidden comedian mimics the official priest'. What we read is therefore the 'partnership of a clown and a preacher' (1967, p. 277). This conclusion forms the basis of Peter Steele's argument that *An Argument* projects Swift as a preacher in motley for whilst sermonising on the (provisional) validity of the status quo, he is taken to delight in the logical extension of that conservatism, the maintenance of 'perfunctory compromise and mutual parasitism' (p. 23). C. N. Manlove stresses the dominance of the 'political motive' behind the Arguer's rhetoric, a secularism all too reminiscent of the Revolution Settlement, for Swift's notion of the 'Country' is constantly pitted against the 'concrete fact of its people' (p. 117). Abstractions are victorious over 'Life'. Fool or Knave, Preacher or Jester, Political Realist or Devout Ingénu—these 'Characters' pulsate under the same authorial skin.

Within a mimetic frame of reference, it would be particularly difficult to better this degree of complex accommodation of opposites. These dichotomies are considered personal, 'logocentric', qualities in Swift's creative psyche. The extent to which they recur in his works most certainly suggests some consistent preoccupations we can call 'Swiftian'. Textually, however, the direction of such enquiries is not in 'Swift's' direction. By 'decentring' the creative subject (the author), it is possible to affix the paired opposites above to rhetorical effects traversed by ideological and transindividual discourses. *An Argument's* split personality is thus an indication of the contradictions within post-Revolution Anglican ideology for which there is little remedy or synthesis. Whilst expressing 'the Trumpery lately written' by Deists aznd Free-Thinkers such as Tindal or Toland, *An Argument* exhibits some of the relief that swimming with an amoral tide might bring. A Deist is correct in pointing out that contemporary respect for the clergy and Gospel teachings as a 'Rule of Faith' is purely nominal. Albeit superficially, we note how the pre-ironic thesis of the text can advance the dictates of the 'Disposition of the World': 'Is not every Body freely allowed to believe whatever he pleaseth; and to publish his Belief to the World whenever he thinks fit; especially if it serve to strengthen the Party which is in the Right?' (II: 29). Advantages to the public involve a denial of the personal reformations that 'real' Christianity brings. A Church that can accommodate Scottish Presbyterians and threaten the continuance of the Test Act (1673) (enforcing attendance at Anglican communion as a prerequisite for public office) is surely prepared to sacrifice the potential disruption that wholesale devotion would bring. The effect is less *ironic* than searchingly realistic. In trying to reform society by his satire, Swift, no doubt testifies unwittingly to his own complicity in its temporising by being unable to offer a clear alternative, things being what they are.

Swift's elusiveness in his most ironic texts has two other results as well, for the full effect of *An Argument* must eventually deprive the reader of any confidence in the status quo at the same time as any confidence in people's capacity to reform themselves by reference to any transcendental ideal. When he disrupts our normal expectations, they can never quite be re-assembled with habitual certainty. If Swift's remedies were plain and readily accessible, if there were not so many rhetorical trap-doors opening under us, our reading habits would be confirmed and also our normal patterns of thought in other matters too. The difference between *An Argument* and *A Project for the Advancement of Religion* is instructive. The latter is surely less arresting and compelling because of its relatively straightforward rhetoric. Swift may despair of some 'airy Imaginations of introducing new Laws for the Amendment of Mankind', but that is only to endorse a perspicuous alternative: 'the due Execution of the old' (II: 61). A critical, and potentially self-reforming, cast of mind is dissolved.

An example of this fruitful strategy of readerly mystification is when the Arguer stigmatises all objectors to Christianity as desiring 'Freedom of Action', the 'Sole End, ... of all Objections':

> And therefore, the Free-Thinkers consider it as a sort of Edifice [Christianity], wherein all the Parts have such a mutual Dependence on each other, that if you happen to pull out one single Nail, the whole Fabrick must fall to the Ground. This was happily expressed by him, who had heard of a Text brought for Proof of the Trinity, which in an antient Manuscript was differently read; he thereupon immediately took the Hint, and by a sudden Deduction of a long *Sorites* [form of dubious syllogistic reasoning based on imprecise terms], most logically concluded; Why, if it be as you say, I may safely whore and drink on, and defy the Parson. (II: 38)

The problems of interpretation here multiply as soon as you conclude that a consistently realised 'character', known perhaps as the Arguer, is responsible for this passage. Frequently, this order of psychological probability is not found. Here the sentiments would seem to be that the destruction of the 'Scheme of the Gospel' is necessary to procure absolute freedom. All the Free-Thinker has to do is to 'pull out one single Nail' and the flimsy structure will collapse. Does Swift imply here that the Gospel message is not constructed of passages that are mutually dependent? Should it be described in the potentially reductive terms of a building? Must the texts containing sacred writ be set above all human interpretation, for fear of attracting the attention of

31

self-interested Deists? Most basic of all, however, is the lack of consistency in having the Arguer describe his rationalising from the 'antient Manuscript' as a *'Sorites'*, a phrase signifying some measure of self-defeating dubiety. F. R. Leavis' distrust of Swift's 'skeletal presence, rigid enough, but without life or body' stems from these moments in Swift's ironic texts where the 'life' of the persona is expressed merely as rhetorical effect, not as an attempt at verisimilitude. Here is Leavis' position on *An Argument*:

> The *Argument Against Abolishing Christianity* and the *Modest Proposal*, for instance, are discussible in the terms in which satire is commonly discussed: as the criticsm of vice, folly, or other aberration, by some kind of reference to positive standards. But even here, even in the *Argument*, where Swift's ironic intensity undeniably directs itself to the defence of something that he is intensely concerned to defend, the effect is essentially negative .... The intensity is purely destructive. (pp. 74–5)

This negative effect, however, has some of the fruitful ambiguity we would expect of the metaphor. A metaphor or symbol is not exactly reducible to a prose paraphrase. If Swift had wanted to produce another *Project for the Advancement of Religion*, we must presume he was free to. Therefore, we cannot refuse to take on board the extra (and perhaps mixed) resonances of the text as it appears because its 'positive standards' reside in rhetorical effects rather than a paraphrasable polemical thesis. Some of the very clearest pieces of writing have the most anaesthetic effects, if the 'positive standards' are obvious and the writer has nothing but impeccable morals to offer.

Swift's eventual indeterminacy of meaning provides further interpretative interest, for the irony, with its features of personae and manipulation of the (desired) reader, discloses certain anxieties concerning the relation between writing and the intention of its writer. Free-thinking, for Swift, meant irresponsible and self-interested nominalism. By reading in the most rational way the writings of the Gospels, they were not only literal-minded and obtuse, but proud and, like Partridge, proclaimed themselves prophets when they were merely possessed by their own fancies. In turn, these fixations were determined by the most basic physical desires and instincts. What operates as a check on these desires is an education in past traditions and Ancient masters, not Modern experimentation.

The Ancients and Moderns Debate And The 1704 Volume

The first thing to comprehend about the English debate between the Ancient and Modern literary aestheticians is that it was not restricted just to art.[7] A faith in the transmission of the best cultural values from the past, usually a definition of the Ancient position, involves the whole world of books, and in any case, art, at this time (as most others), was often taken to be a reliable indication of political, ethical and even mental health as well as literary craft. We have already seen how Locke could be alarmed at the capricious association thoughts could form because of their basis in experience. How much more was this the case with words. Denis Donoghue's description of Swift's style in *The Drapier's Letters* (1724–25), that it was 'for use rather than adornment, a style of russet and kersey' (p. 159), could be applied to much of his unparodic work. This is a style framed constantly to the present context, as its aim is to persuade a particular audience about a localised issue. This does need to be emphasised when Swift is recognised as an Ancient writer. However, as we have seen in *The Contests and Dissentions*, such issues were often present to Swift as reincarnations of much older contexts. *The Battel of the Books*, for example, whilst

33

addressing itself to literary disputes of the 1690s is also an accomplished attempt at a mock-heroic allegory. Virgil's books wage war with Dryden's, for example, on Ancient Soil. Similarly, in *An Argument*, the threat of a sudden resurgence of *'real'* Christianity 'would be full as absurd as the Proposal of *Horace*, where he advises the *Romans*, all in a Body, to leave their City, and seek a new Seat in some remote Part of the World, by Way of Cure for the Corruption of their Manners' (II: 27–8). Swift's instinct is often to establish parallels and analogues even if in jest. The Teller of *A Tale of a Tub*, who is confident he is expressing new truths in a new style, just publicises his own ignorance. The topical and the precedent could therefore coexist in Swift's writing for they seem to exist in an intimate relationship.

Even in Temple's work, however, the legacy of the past could appear threatening as well as helpful. Whilst a new creative artist was inevitably nourished by the works of antiquity, (s)he was at the same time aware of a debt that tended to constrict and inhibit such novelty. Temple's *Essay* forms a powerful argument more against Modern *scientific* optimism, especially if it spreads to the humanities. He contrasts the legions of 'Scribblers . . ., that like Mushrooms or Flys are born and dye in small circles of time' with those 'Books, [which] like Proverbs, receive their Chief Value from the Stamp and Esteem of Ages through which they have passed' (Spingarn, III: 34). This resolve is shaken on the other hand, when he turns to the possibility of, and motive for, new works. Account needs to be taken of the 'weight and number of so many other mens thoughts and notions' which may 'suppress' or 'hinder' the free play of mind 'from which all Invention arises; As heaping on Wood or too many Sticks, or too close together, suppresses and sometimes quite extinguishes a little spark that would otherwise have grown up to a noble flame' (Spingarn, III: 48). This is presented as an incipient weakness of Modernity but it is also acknowledged as caused by a faulty recognition and use of classical knowledge, fuel sometimes too close-packed and numerous to do more than suffocate the present.

This unthinking classicism Swift felt as deficient in judgement. The 'great . . . Lover of Antiquities' who writes Swift's *Tritical Essay upon the Faculties of the Mind* (1711) has too great a veneration for his commonplace-book, for whilst claiming to avoid 'stale Topicks and thread-bare Quotations', he provides a muddled mosaic of proverbs and dicta that proves his unsuitability for the task (I: 246). The Ancient position is not to honour tradition uncritically. The most immediate targets of the 1704 volume were not, indeed, Modern wits but the editor–critics, William Wotton and Richard Bentley, whose scholarship and enthusiasm for Modern advances in geometry and experimental science Swift preferred to describe as pedantry—system instead of spirit. In this, the Ancient Schoolmen could be as blind as the Moderns, as Swift makes plain in his *Ode to the Honourable Sir William Temple* (written 1692–93; published 1745):

> They purchase knowledge at the expense
> Of common breeding, common sense,
> And at once grow scholars and fools; . . .
> (ll.42–4, p. 56)

It is not necessarily inconsistent of Swift, therefore, in *The Battel of the Books*, to describe Temple as both an Ancient and a Modern in the same sentence, he, 'having been educated and long conversed among the *Antients*, was, of all the *Moderns*, their greatest Favourite, and became their greatest Champion' (I: 147). Modernity in this case is attuned both to the 'common forms' and their traditional foundation.

We have already seen how Swift's hopes for Anglicanism were often based on its power to act as a unifying force transcending accidents of time or place. The Bee in debate with the methodical and self-sufficient spider in the *Battel* grants the latter's 'method and Art' whilst perceiving that the 'Materials' were 'nought' and not calculated for 'Duration' (I: 149). By pursuing analytical rigour and the narrow rules of logic Swift felt that something inexpressibly human was being squeezed out, a prelude to a new barbarism. The Spider 'whose Spoils lay scattered before the Gates of his Palace, like human Bones before the Cave of some Giant' cannot live up to such heroic afflatus. His web, which Swift transforms into a 'Castle . . . Cittadel' or 'Fortress', can be breached simply by the Bee's alighting on one of the 'outward walls' (I: 147–8). Similarly, when this 'Hero' is granted speech, it issues forth as disconnected expletives and idiomatic ephemera. This episode makes it easier to believe the 'Ancient' Scaliger when he reproves Bentley for a '*Learning*' that has made him more '*Barbarous*' and a 'Study of *Humanity*' that has made him more '*Inhuman*' (I: 161). A world of books and nothing else is a danger.

The World of Print and the Teller's lack of Authority

A *Tale of a Tub* is one of the most self-conscious pieces of writing. The Teller's desperate desire to please his readers by incessantly putting them in the picture so determines the mood of the writing that it usurps what would seem to be its main function: to tell a tale. Even when the reader has accepted this reversal of expectation (s)he has to identify not only who is speaking but to whom it is all addressed. Protestations of the warmth or potential antagonism between writer and reader are repeatedly offered by the Teller, to such an extent that such assumed intimacy and attempts at artistic control become self-defeating. The Teller cannot convince us of his *ethos* or *artistic* presence because he desires the reader to be so assured of his *physical* existence. Disorder results and in turn we sense the fragility of any writer–reader relationship.

Ironic works cannot say exactly what they mean. A reader is obliged to deduce, at one remove, some original intention and so identify the boundary between irony and direct statement. The mere fact that *A Tale of a Tub* is so full of possibilities is both confusing *and* liberating. Frequently the enjoyment in reading the *Tale* stems from its lack of decorum and direction. Any recognition that it should really be endorsing distaste at the 'numerous and gross Corruptions in Religion and Learning' (I: 1) and that Swift's ideal of 'correct' form involved coherent interrelations of content and a plain, unvarnished expression can be corroborated by other texts such as *A Proposal for Correcting, Improving and Ascertaining the English Tongue* or the orderly and plain polemic of *The Publick Spirit of the Whigs* (1714) but, first, they are by no means contemporary documents, and, secondly, give no clear evidence whey *they* should be preferred as authoritative guides to the 'real' Jonathan Swift. The truth may be that we instinctively read a plain style as neutral and unironic work as revelatory. Even the indication of the *Tale*'s satiric targets, those 'Corruptions in Religion and Learning', cannot be relied on totally both because the phrase comes in the 'Apology', not added until the fifth edition (1710), and also because its unironic qualities by no means stand out distinctly from its ironies. For instance, although the 'Apology' offers a defence of the positive ethics of the *Tale* against the critics of its first edition, it also bears several resemblances to the self-apologies of more ironic positions. Compare his description of the 'Swift' of the 1690s:

> He was then a young Gentleman much in the World, and wrote to the Tast of those who were like himself; therefore in order to allure them, he gave a Liberty to his Pen, which might not suit with maturer Years, or graver Characters, and which he could

have easily corrected with a very few Blots, had he been master of
his Papers for a Year or two before their Publication. (I: 1–2)

with the Teller's conclusion:

In my Disposure of Employments of the Brain, I have thought fit
to make *Invention* the *Master*, and to give *Method* and *Reason*, the
Office of its *Lacquays*. The Cause of this Distribution was, from
observing it my peculiar Case, to be often under a Temptation of
being *Witty*, upon Occasions, where I could be neither *Wise* nor
Sound, nor anything to the Matter in hand. And, I am too much a
Servant of the *Modern* Way, to neglect any such Opportunities,
whatever Pains or Improprieties I may be at, to introduce them.
(I: 134)

Does the 'Swift' of 1710 regard the 'Swift' of 1696–97 as a
'Modern'? What is more, the 'Apology' deploys several
dubious arguments to acquit Swift of full authorial
responsibility. The text, for example, has not been
authorised. There should have been four 'wooden Machines'
for oratory in the 'Introduction' and not three. 'Those who
had the Papers in their Power' had censored such a quantity
because it 'had something in it of Satyr' (I: 4). Further
corrections could have been made if he had had his papers
recently in his possession (I: 5). The 'Original Copy' had not
so many 'Chasms', or hiatuses, as actually appear (I: 9). This
was to become a familiar device of Swift's, for it highlights
one of the 'Modern' writer's greatest problems: how to
maintain one's authority over the *printed* word. In handing
over one's manuscript to a bookseller (today's publisher) the
more personal contact between writer and reader that the pen
and one's long-hand script invited was dissolved. The
mediation of the printing-press did not necessarily ensure
clarity or even a desirable measure of survival for one's
thoughts. In 'living' speech the speaker can clarify and refine
his/her concepts in response to an identifiable audience. The

printed word may bear the same marks of the author's possession, but these are nominal compared with the speaker's power to retract, qualify and employ physical indicators (facial expression, posture of the body or gestures) to create his/her own context. The only context for the printed *Tale* is the *individual* reader, with all his/her possibly accidental and uncharted interpretative powers confronted by printer's ink and paper, relics of 'the Original Copy', not only the physical substance that lands on the bookseller's desk, but also the primordial ideas that spring from the writer's intellect. Communication is a desperately vulnerable quality once it becomes a commodity.[8]

This is not to say that the text we have now is a botched job. New editions were published very quickly (the second and third in 1704 and fourth in 1705), and, consequently, it would have been quite possible for Swift to intervene before 1710 if the published text had been seriously defective. Therefore, the 'chasms' as we have them seem desperate measures on the Teller's part to edge the argument out of an uncomfortable corner. When attempting a grand interpretative scheme of 'Oratorial Receptacles', he resorts to the printing-press's equivalent of an embarrassed silence when he is stuck for a symbolic link between a ladder and '*Faction*' (I: 37). The same measures are taken when he tries to account for the 'fountains of *Enthusiasm*' and how they can be so variously diverted or dammed 'as to be the sole Point of Individuation between *Alexander the Great, Jack of Leyden*, and Monsieur *Des Cartes*':

> The present Argument is the most abstracted that ever I engaged in, it strains my Faculties to their highest Stretch; and I desire the Reader to attend with utmost Perpensity; For, I now proceed to unravel this knotty Point.
> There is in Mankind a certain******************************
> **

Hic Multa   **
desiderantur **
    And this I take to be a clear solution of the Matter. (I:
    107).

No wonder that the Teller cannot come up with such a
'clear Solution'. The burden of the argument has certainly
been to deny any great difference between system-builders at
all. Those who live by method get taken over by it and
individuality fades. Even then, such methods seem much
brighter in prospect than in their fruition. As Bickerstaff
helped expose in reference to Partridge's astrology, reality is
unencompassable. Those who attempt to tame it by 'clear
Solutions' implicate themselves in the reductive anarchy of
Man's fallen nature. Mysteries have to be revealed by God.
    Such jokes at the Teller's expense do not quite disperse
our consciousness of Swift's anxieties in writing for the
press. Once published, the written word is exposed to the
merciless possibilities of misinterpretation, both by mistake
and partisan calculation. In Gulliver's visit to the academy at
Lagado the School of 'political Projectors' is not over nice
about the intentions or good faith of those they suspect.
Plots may be discovered by learning of their suspects' diets
and qualitative analysis of their faeces. Gulliver informs
them (in a passage much softened from the first and second
editions) that such a school has an equivalent in 'Langden'
(England) whereby the most innocent letters once 'delivered
to a set of Artists very dextrous in finding out the
mysterious Meanings of Words, Syllables and Letters' can
be deciphered as seditious and so, treasonable (XII: 190–2).
Good motives are not enough.
    Pedantic interpretations are almost as bad. Wotton and
Bentley, by missing the point of the texts they edit, bury the
true meaning as effectively as if they wilfully misrepresented
it. For the 1710 edition, Swift included the plentiful

annotation that most modern texts now include, incorporating *verbatim* some of Wotton's own comments from his *A Defense of the Reflections upon Ancient and Modern Learning, In Answer to the Objections of Sir W. Temple, and Others. With Observations upon The Tale of a Tub* (1705). The result is to ensure, by typographical means, a reader's already willing distraction from what is in the body of the piece. (The fact that the main text is already a hopelessly entangled web only intensifies the comedy rather than defeats it.) Such annotation, so studious and plodding, can often counterpoint or enact the Teller's own preoccupations. For example, the Teller's fear that no new material for panegyric writing can now exist receives tacit confirmation from the margins of the page:

Plutarch   He may ring the Changes as far as it will go, and vary his Phrase till he has talk'd round; but the Reader quickly finds, it is all Pork, with a little variety of Sawce: For there is no inventing Terms of Art beyond our Idea's; and when Idea's are exhausted, Terms of Art must be so too. (I: 30)

This is the victory of editor over writer. The Teller's failure of the imagination stems from the erosive anxiety that Art is determined totally by its Ideas. (This is, however, not quite true of the *effect* of the *Tale.*) The only metaphor for this construction is found in Plutarch, a reference which in turn embodies the problem graphically. Well might the Teller conclude that to 'write upon Nothing' is the only experiment open to the Modern author, to 'let the Pen still move on' even when the 'subject is utterly exhausted' (I: 133).

The Teller's writing marks the advent of not only a mass audience but also the printed word as marketable object. The Teller's massive inferiority complex manifests itself in the intense desire to buttonhole the reader, and so be heard above the crowd. He is, however, eventually defeated by the presence of the past, whilst striving defiantly to do without it. The question still to be resolved is: does Swift see himself in a similar predicament or is he merely undermining the inept Modern modes of over-familiarity and self-exposure, from which he naturally exempts himself? This has divided criticism of the *Tale* into two camps, the one stressing the culpability of the Teller and the artistry of the omniscient Swift,[9] the other seeing in the *Tale*'s desperate humour Swift's exploration of tensions otherwise inexpressible by the Anglican clergyman. The former position is a mimetic one, the latter textual.

To Swift, the world of print, whilst not totally new, must have seemed very much a contemporary phenomenon. As Terry Belanger has recently pointed out, the expiry of the Licensing Act in 1695 freed many printers from central control but it also denied writers copyright protection (Rivers, p. 10). Even with the Copyright Act (1709) the detection of infringement was limited. In short, print could proliferate and, with this increase of printed matter, an author's authority over his (printed) words was limited. In the face of a defensive cooperation between booksellers, a writer's words could be owned quite literally by his/her publisher. On top of that, a Modern had the daunting prospect of Ancient examples continually before him/her during much of a formal literary education. The literary result of these gradual trends was the professionalisation of the writer. Hugh Kenner demonstrated in 1964 how Swift's distrust of print led him to 'emphasize to the point of grotesqueness exactly those features which distinguish the printed book *per se*, the printed book as technological artifact, from a human document'. The writer, as a figure within his own creation or as presupposed by it, was not so much exiled as generalised. 'He is the obedient humble servant of whatever reader is jackass enough to find him congenial' (pp. 37–8). Denis Donoghue agrees, and takes issue with Irvin Ehrenpreis' reduction of the irony to what

Swift 'must have meant':

> We should not assume, reading the *Tale*, that the words are primarily designed to carry the voice of a single indentifiable speaker. We are reading words on a page; implying rather things being said than a voice saying them . . . the 'author' is the anonymous slave of print; 'he' is as servile as the printed page . . . Mr. Ehrenpreis takes the words in one sense only, as the transcript of a man's speech, so he can do nothing with them except, moment by moment, trace them back to their presumed origin. He does not allow for the fact that words are exerted upon their object, regardless of their mere source. (pp. 8–9).

The Teller is, if any entity, Anon, *any* teller of a printed tale. This textual interest does not depend on our identifying a consistent perspective, a personality onto which we can unload our guilt.

This reading of the *Tale* has not gone unchallenged. As John R. Clark has pointed out, the rhetorical emphases of New Critical works substitute the coherence of a persona for that of the author. Satire's power of persuasion thus stems from a 'personality' consistently, or gradually felt to be, in the wrong; we lose trust in what the persona signifies and thus embrace its implied opposite. Clark's reading of the *Tale* strips the Teller of his Modernity. The effort at novel wit and paradox is merely the provison of 'stale and trite epideictic and forensic paradoxes in a long and tired tradition [the conceits of the early seventeeth century] ... Swift presents to us a Modern who, intending to be original, paradoxically is traditional' (p. 194). In arguing that New Critical readings, such as Miriam Starkman's and Ronald Paulson's do not take sufficient account of the paradoxes and inhumanity of the persona,[10] Clark still keeps faith with a 'mimetic' model: one that, even if superficially irregular to the point of a paradoxical persona, can still recognise 'that plot or action is the crucial framework upon which all else

43

depends—a plot whose regular advancement raises the action to a climax and creates a totality by that action's very movement from beginning to middle to end' (p. xiii). This may be sophisticated, but it still relies on a 'presumed origin'.

More directly antagonistic to Donoghue's reading are those readers who are not persona critics and who attempt to trace Swift's hand throughout. Sir Herbert Davis' review of Paulson's study (1961) displayed irritation at the 'wretched Hack' constantly interposed between Swift and the readers of the *Tale*. Gardner Stout, Jr, in 1969, even directed a dramatic excerpt for us: 'In telling his *Tale of a Tub*, Swift acts out the vices of the mob before the delighted eyes of his elite audience. The *Tale*'s rhetoric generally suggests an image of Swift, sitting with his fellow wits in an Augustan drawing-room' where they listen to 'a master mimic and parodist.'[11] The pertinence of the (obviously) printed medium to the effect of the *Tale* seems lost on Stout at this point. For Robert Elliott, whilst it may seem obvious, even tautological, to point out that there can be no voice other than the author's in a literary work, the term 'voice' seems fraught with the wrong connotations: 'What we have are silent words on a printed page, but our metaphors retain the sense of persons speaking. . . . We find it hard to speak of the actions of the printed page without recourse to terms from the pre-Gutenberg era' [that is, before printing] (p. 109). Elliott's exhaustive survey describes a persistent dilemma for the mimetic critic: having assembled the mass of factual evidence that locates Swift within his society and his epoch, does this oblige him/her to find the 'central' thread of coherence (a plot or 'action') that best fits such information, or are these historical/sociological factors peripheral? The problem is really one of relevance. Our desire to identify the 'authentic' voice could really be a form of deliberate blindness to a text's full complexity. However, as Elliott points out, our present critical vocabulary is not geared to such complexity, especially when the usual role of the satirist is as a polemicist, preferring the light of ethical day to the dark of psychic night. As Elliott also points out, 'in one sense every character in a created work speaks for the author; that is, each is an agency through whom the author speaks' (p. 112). The problem is that the *Tale* provides only an implied framework whereby these 'characters' may be ranked and interpreted.

Metaphor and Madness in the Tale

As we have seen, Swift's more public statements on language and style were at odds with his practice. Whilst favouring 'simplicity', texts such as the *Tale* or *Gulliver* are anything but simple, not just in their larger rhetorical strategies but also in more local shifts of decorum or, in Smith's phrase, their 'lexical fields' (pp. 49-69). An *Argument* can be interpreted, if clarity is our goal, as a swingeing indictment of Free-Thinkers and the time-serving clergy who provide them with such an opportune target. The decision to rest there is that of a 'mimetic' critic. The 'textual' critic must be prepared to observe all the contradictions without making too narrow a choice of those of which Swift 'must have' been aware.

So various is the *Tale* in its digressions (not just those announced in chapter-headings) that it forces interpretative choice on the reader. The first problem is to choose where the *Tale* starts: at section II, or at the 'Apology', or at the 'Bookseller's' dedication to Somers? Similarly, the tale proper would seem to be that of the three brothers and their father's will. From section II it proceeds in alternation with the 'Digressions' until at section VIII (just after the 'Digression in Praise of Digressions') the Aeolist episode halts the narrative flow and the reader notes more resemblance to a 'Digression' in this section than to the tale. Perhaps here our reading recognises that the 'Digressions' are as central as the tale. Consequently, when events proceed once more with section XI and Jack's use of the will, *narrative* coherence is not so significant as less linear unities: both how the Teller's obtrusive garrulity relates to the fable of the brothers and also what might be the possible significance of such garish revelations of self.

Erasmus' *Praise of Folly* (1511), which is one of the most direct sources for the *Tale*, has Folly claim that she is one of the few figures 'whose divine powers can gladden the hearts of gods and men' (p. 63). Propriety can be thrown to the winds when she is in the company, for she always likes the extempore mode of life the best, free of calculation and judgement. Folly's good humour, however, can modulate to a less equable key. In Chapter 31, the pitiful and grotesque join her company, desperately eager to preserve their illusions. Folly entertains such cosmetics as dyeing white hair, wearing wigs or borrowing teeth, even from a pig (p. 109). This wild and whirling pageant is not, however, the whole story. As Everett Zimmerman points out, Folly's sophistries are obvious: 'She engages attention by her assaults on logic and the cleverness of her stratagems. But as she undermines the pretenses of wisdom, the small truths that she entraps in her equivocations loom large' (p. 74). Erasmus' Folly gives herself away yet this is not self-defeating because, dressed in motley, the cracks in her argument can be papered over with gladsome wit. Besides, religious abuses are clearly highlighted at the work's conclusion; the reader returns from a feast of fools to confront sterner fare. Swift's 'Folly' is, however, Madness and the return to normality, constituted as a voice identifiable as the author's, is constantly thwarted.

The most recent criticism of the *Tale* has highlighted its

manic undecipherability as a problem not only of deciding where Swift stands but also how the reader constructs his/her own perspective as well.[12] As interpretation of the basic satiric context is problematic (such as, what is being attacked and on what authority), most textual critics have concluded that the main point of the *Tale* is to demonstrate the extreme difficulty of interpreting anything without a divine yardstick. Even then, as the brothers' treatment of their father's will testifies, any writ, however sacred, can be misread due to human wilfulness. The fixations that seduce judgement are not just located in the Teller. As Partridge's example makes clear, Swift had no confidence in humanity's grasp of the most self-evident 'common forms'.

The Teller's madness is on the other hand a specific disorder. Not only is he incapable of framing his words to match what he wants to say, the reader cannot be sure just what that exactly is. He suggests indeed that the work has no other function than to divert rationalists or wits from picking 'Holes in the weak sides of Religion and Government'. By diverting the reader, potential iconoclasts are similarly distracted. The Teller is assigned such a task by a 'Grand Committee', one of whose number, a 'certain curious and refined Observer', remembers that whales are sometimes muddled in pursuit of a ship by the sailors throwing out to it an empty tub which the whale tosses about instead:

> This Parable was immediately mythologiz'd: The *Whale* was interpreted to be *Hobbes's Leviathan* which tosses and plays with all other Schemes of Religion and Government, whereof a great many are hollow, and dry, and empty, and noisy, and wooden, and given to Rotation ... The *Ship* in danger, is easily understood to be its old Antitype the *Commonwealth*. But how to analyze the *Tub*, was a Matter of difficulty; when after long Enquiry and Debate, the literal Meaning was preserved. (I: 24)

Preserving the 'literal meaning' is in effect, an admission of failure on the interpreter's part, a failure of his systems of analysis to convert all the terms of his metaphor into significant meaning. The *Tale* similarly resists such orderly reduction. In itself it is empty, but what it enacts and signifies is packed with force and suggestive possibilities. The failure of the Teller's aims is far more arresting than their realisation could ever have been.

At the root of the Teller's troubles lies his inability to master language and its power to suggest as well as denote. 'Schemes of Religion and Government' suggest to the Teller forms of hollowness, in that they promise more than they accomplish. Increasingly, however, such 'hollowness' begins to provide the Teller with the terms in which he continues his interpretation, at the expense of casting greater light on the 'Schemes' originally described. Thus, 'hollowness' leads to 'dry', 'empty', 'noisy', 'wooden' and—'rotation'. In what sense do such 'schemes' rotate? A tub rotates when tossed on the ocean; any scheme can only do so metaphorically. Association has triumphed over elucidation, the 'transforming imagination' over judgement. Metaphors lose their power to describe and become opaque. The 'Ambition to be heard in a Crowd' is satisfied by *physical* elevation alone, from pulpit, ladder or '*Stage-Itinerant*' (I: 34), Lord Peter decrees that '"a Slice from a Twelve-penny loaf"' is '"true, good natural Mutton as any in *Leaden-Hall* Market"' (I: 73) and Jack use his father's will as a 'Night-cap' or an 'Umbrello in rainy weather', this despite 'not daring to let slip a Syllable without its authority' (I: 122). This incompetence is so persistent that the Teller *and* his creations, Peter and Jack, are deemed, not just bad writers, but mad as well.

For both rationalist and empiricist philosophers of the seventeenth century, a clinical definition of madness was an impossibility. Descartes regarded dreams together with all forms of error as beyond the pale of reason. In his *Discourse on Method* (1637), the attempt to understand the 'ground of our opinions' involved such slow progress and such circumspection that it resembled 'walking alone and in the dark', an insurance against 'falling'. Indeed, his third guideline in this project was to commence with 'objects the simplest and easiest to know' and thence to build up a picture of the most complex objects of thought 'assigning in thought a certain order even to those objects which in their own nature do not stand in a relation of antecedence and sequence' (pp. 14–16). Method (at all costs) was the only criterion of sanity and a resistance to the whims of custom. Hobbes went even further in claiming that 'Passions unguided, are for the most part meere Madnesse' (Part 1, Ch. 8, p. 142). The secret, unuttered thoughts that flutter around one's brain would be proof of insanity if given utterance just in the order in which they occur. 'Without Steddinesse and Direction to some End, a great Fancy is one kind of Madnesse; such as they have, that entring into any discourse, are snatched from their purpose, by every thing that comes in their thought, into so many, and so long digressions' (1, 8, p. 136). The judgement is needed to sift those sentiments to be uttered, requisite to the 'Time, Place, and Persons', from those 'extravagant, and pleasant fancies' which could only appear 'as if a man, from being tumbled into the dirt, should come and present himselfe before good company' (1, 8, p. 137). Although Swift distrusted the mechanical aspects of Cartesian method and Hobbesian psychology, he also sympathised with these fears about the dark underside of human motives. Both Jack and the Teller tumble in the dirt to disgust the reader.[13] The problem with most readings nowadays is that such disgust also breeds a grim fascination. Like some Augustans who paid to gawp at the spiritually deranged in Bedlam, we can also finds such abnormality both threatening and diverting. In the Teller's case, such diversion calls in question that state of being from which we

49

are being diverted. 'Steddinesse and Direction' should be *our* aim in reading the *Tale*. The trouble is that the object of such decisiveness always proves a mirage; the reader is destined not to find a clear path through the *Tale* on the Teller's terms. (S)he experiences instead a less easily defined frustration and bewilderment as a result of the very act of reading Swift's 'narrative'.

The earliest critics of the *Tale* have often been regarded as blind to Swift's satirical intention, in that they often refused to recognise the honourable motives that underlay the surface anarchy. Dr William King, in *Some Remarks on A Tale of a Tub* (1704), felt that it exceeded 'all bounds of modesty' (*CH*, p. 33). Wotton believed that, in the *Tale*, all ethics and industry were 'made a May-Game' (*CH*, p. 38), whereas Sir Richard Blackmore, in his *Essay upon Wit* (1716), notes an 'abuse of Wit' where the author had been 'pleasant with the Principles of a Christian' (*CH*, p. 52). Such readings refuse to see past the indecorous surface where Swift forces us to experience, at such length, the 'May-Game' of his text. In the 'Digression concerning Madness', we are taken on a tour of Bedlam, meeting one who 'has forgot the common *Meaning* of Words, but an admirable Retainer of the *Sound*' next to, and on a par with, one who rakes in his own dung and, indeed, feeds on it and, finally a 'Student' who turns out to be a '*Taylor* run made with Pride'. These emblems of irrationality depict figures who live in their own worlds and who are inspired purely by their own fancies. This pageant seems at a safe distance, and yet Swift's work brings the scene uncomfortably close. The '*Taylor*' who 'holds you out his Hand to Kiss' is found to be 'adorned with many other Qualities, upon which, at present, I shall not farther enlarge. .*Heark in your Ear* .... I am strangely mistaken, if all his Address, his Motions, and his Airs, would not then be very natural, and in their proper Element' (I: 112–13). Is the italicised phrase the Teller's or the Tailor's, suddenly confronting the reader by stepping outside the safely insulated literary framework? It could be, however, that the Teller and Tailor are one and the same and that 'the other Qualities' the 'Student' possesses are snares to trap the reader into concluding that fixated derangement is 'natural' and that he and the reader share 'their proper Element'—by now, the Bedlam we have toured for the past two or three pages.

The reader cannot avoid being implicated in such descriptions, and such indecorum no doubt troubled contemporary readers. So unregulated is the Teller's invention and wit that it exemplifies the dangers Locke felt proceeded from 'metaphor and allusion', the arena where wit assembles ideas 'with quickness and variety, wherein can be found any resemblance or congruity, thereby to make up pleasant pictures and agreeable visions in the fancy'. The judgement's power to make careful distinctions, 'to avoid being misled by similitude' (II, xi, vol. 1, p. 123), is not, however, why the *Tale* is now read. The 'common forms' with which Martin keeps faith are relatively colourless compared with the idiosyncrasies of Peter and Jack. As John Traugott points out, Martin appears a mere 'manikin' next to Jack and Peter who 'appear finally not as exceptions to the rule of life but the rule itself' (Rawson 1983, p. 124). What is more, the *Tale* takes us beyond this potentially disturbing conclusion, for the very appeal of the work stems from the rapid excursions of allusion and metaphor, sometimes unprompted by some clear referent, that the Teller deploys. Mimetically, Swift seems to steer a middle course between the 'peaceful Possession' of 'Credulity' and the rationalist who is primed 'with Tools for cutting, and opening, and mangling, and piercing' (I: 109). Textually, the reader experiences the world of the Tale as populated with the most uncommon forms, most of which detain the eye and cannot be easily shunned.

51

The Teller, once a member of Bedlam (I: 11) and writing merely as a form of therapy (I: 114), can still write a true word in jest. Swift's model in this was not just Erasmus, but also Michel Montaigne, whose *Essays* (1580) accept the disorderly tendencies that attend all attempts at self-discovery. Definition, both verbal and philosphical, is often merely a desperate attempt to hold at bay the heterogeneity of life. In his essay 'On Experience' (Book III, Chapter 13), Montaigne believes that all interpretation confident of clearing up doubt is doomed to failure. The rule of life is to live according to the simplicities of nature which teach us humanity (p. 403). Contradiction is Man's birthright, Montaigne's especially, for whilst he can claim that the mind's 'food is wonder, search, and ambiguity' (p. 348), a few pages later he regards plainness as true wisdom: 'Oh, how soft and pleasant and healthful a pillow, whereon to rest a prudent head, is ignorance and lack of curiosity!' (p. 354). Of the two alternatives, however, the text *enacts* the former delight in process rather than product. The same can be said of Swift's *Tale*. Any serenity ensured by some cut-and-dried conclusion is often overturned around the next corner or by what it has just passed.

Therefore, when we arrive at the Teller's conclusion that the 'Philosopher or Projector' who can 'Sodder and patch up the Flaws and Imperfection's of Nature' deserves well of mankind, our assent is sapped by the shock of the flayed woman and anatomised beau of a few lines before. The two perceptions should be working in tandem, for the philosophic serenity of the conclusion could be enforced by the distasteful analysis we have just read. We could choose to be foolish and innocent, content with a patched and papered nature; the problem is, it can now *only* be viewed as a façade. Knowledge cannot be wished away. Claude Rawson reads the woman and beau as 'momentary intensities which do not merely *serve* the argument they are meant to illustrate, but actually *spill over it*'. This suddenness and its brevity occur 'outside the expectations of the immediate logic' and leave a trace of cruel fantasy (1973, p. 34). Nowhere in Montaigne is such *textual* dissonance experienced.

Swift's earliest writing often demonstrates a radical uncertainty that Donoghue noted as residing in an effect on the reader rather than an ascertainable possession of Swift or even deducible from some projected persona. The 'meaning' of a text like the *Tale* or *An Argument* cannot be adequately paraphrased as it springs from the experience of following the light and shade of Rawson's 'momentary intensities'. What makes the *Tale* quite so worrying, however, is its invitation to share these as natural. Madness before the Age of Reason was typified by Michel Foucault (in 1961) as a Ship of Fools, a voyage of discovery in a darkness external to Man. Gradually, reason establishes such dominance that it can confine madness within the mental hospital. The divinely touched Fool of *King Lear*, for example, would become a Bedlam spectacle: 'madness no longer lies in wait for mankind at the four corners of the earth; it insinuates itself within man, or rather it is a subtle rapport that man maintains with himself.'[14] By grappling with unreason the *Tale* offers no comfortable conclusions for its readers, unless they remain blind to its textual complexities and, what is more, to the ambivalences awakened in us by them.

Notes

1. The sources for this position are discussed by F. P. Lock (1983), pp. 146–61.
2. Swift's distaste for 'Free-Thinking' is best illustrated by turning to his parody of Anthony Collins' *Discourse of Free-Thinking* (1713) whose arguments supported the free exercise of reason

in religious matters, even when it contradicted clerical guidance. *Mr. Collins's Discourse on Free-Thinking* (1713, IV: 23–48) set up the Natural against the Dutiful: 'no Religion whatsoever contributes in the least to mend Mens Lives' (IV: 41).

3. The degree of Swift's indebtedness is not clear. The fullest account is given by A. C. Elias, Jr, *Swift at Moor Park: Problems in Biography and Criticism* (Philadelphia, 1982), pp. 155–200 (especially pp. 157–72, where Temple is regarded as a butt of the *Tale*'s 'Digression on Madness'). See also John Traugott's comments (Rawson, 1983, pp. 90–100), and Downie's alternative view (pp. 32–53).

4. Probyn (1978a), pp. 43–56; Smith, especially pp. 27–47.

5. For Mandeville's effect on early eighteenth-century thought, see M. M. Goldsmith, 'Public Virtue and Private Vices: Bernard Mandeville and English Political Ideologies in the Early Eighteenth Century', *Eighteenth-Century Studies* (1975–76), 477–510.

6. For further description of contemporary linguistic theory, see Murray Cohen, *Sensible Words: Linguistic Practice in England, 1640–1785* (Baltimore, 1977).

7. See Clark, pp. 83–115.

8. See Martha Woodmansee, 'The Genius and the Copyright: Economic and Legal Conditions of the Emergence of the "Author" ', *Eighteenth-Century Studies* (1984), 425–48.

9. This is the view of Martin C. Battestin: 'Swift's method is obliquely to endorse the order of things by exposing to our view the image and consequences of disorder, both the nature of confusion and its form' (*The Providence of Wit: Aspects of Form in Augustan Literature and the Arts* [Oxford, 1974], p. 240).

10. Miriam Starkman, *Swift's Satire on Learning in 'A Tale of a Tub'* (Princeton, N.J., 1950); Ronald Paulson, *Theme and Structure in Swift's 'A Tale of a Tub'* (New Haven, N.Y., 1960).

11. Sir Herbert Davis, *Review of English Studies* (1961), 301; Gardner Stout, Jr, 'Speaker and Satiric Vision in Swift's *A Tale of a Tub*', *Eighteenth-Century Studies* (1969), 183.

12. This is the central thesis of Frances Louis' study (especially pp. 45–54) where reading the *Tale* and the *Travels* is primarily an epistemological problem (that is, a constant questioning, and anxiety about, our bases for knowledge). Interpretation is

also seen as the 'subject' of the *Tale* in Smith, pp. 125–44, Korkowski, pp. 403–8, Zimmerman (in relation to the rise in Protestant Biblical interpretation), pp. 39-60, and Atkins *passim* ('Swift nowhere in the *Tale* suggests any hope that plain and clear language will yield unequivocal meaning. Rather, he focuses on the ways by which even supposedly plain meanings are abused, converted, and willfully misread' [p. 109]).

13. Swift echoes Hobbes in his *Some Thoughts on Free-Thinking* (c. 1713; published 1767), when he quotes a 'prelate of the kingdom of Ireland' who defines a madman as one who 'spoke out whatever came into his mind, and just in the confused manner as his imagination presented the ideas'. Furthermore, 'if the wisest man' uttered his thoughts in a 'crude, indigested manner, as they came into his head', he would inevitably be regarded as 'raving mad' (IV: 49).

14. *Madness and Civilization: A History of Insanity in the Age of Reason* (English edn, trans. Richard Howard, 1967), p. 26.

3

Gulliver

My Father had a small Estate in *Nottinghamshire*; I was the Third of five Sons. He sent me to *Emanuel-College* in *Cambridge*, at Fourteen Years old, where I resided three Years, and applied my self close to my Studies: But the Charge of maintaining me (although I had a very scanty Allowance) being great for a narrow Fortune; I was bound Apprentice to Mr. *James Bates*, an eminent surgeon in *London*, with whom I continued four Years; and my Father now and then sending me small Sums of Money, I laid them out in learning Navigation, and other Parts of the Mathematicks, useful to those who intend to travel, as I always believed it would be some time or other my Fortune to do. (XI: 19)

This is not our first introduction to Lemuel Gulliver. In the first editions of 1726 and 1727, his 'antient and intimate Friend' and publisher, Richard Sympson, speaks at first on his behalf, commending his 'plain and simple' style and only regretting that he, 'after the Manner of Travellers, is a little too circumstantial'. This is an error in the right direction, however, for Sympson observes how there is 'an Air of

56

Truth apparent through the whole', and also how much Gulliver was 'distinguished for his Veracity'. This sense of his sobriety would seem to have survived his drastic alteration after the voyage to Houynhynmland, for, now retired, out of the public's gaze 'near Newark', he is still 'in good Esteem among his Neighbours' (XI: 9). Come 1735 and the third volume of Swift's *Works*, however, and two further items of prefatory material provide a rather different testimonial. 'Capt.' Gulliver provides the reader with a letter to Sympson and there is also a short 'Advertisement'. As with the *Tale*, Swift's editorial additions do not always clarify our reading of the main text. In this case, however, our view of the apparently open-handed and equable writer of the first chapter is surely rendered ambiguous much sooner. In earlier editions, Gulliver cannot immediately be distinguished from other travellers whose observations on foreign exotica had the force of fact. The 1735 additions not only question the accuracy of the spelling (a relatively minor editorial matter and one of Swift's facetious glances at editorial pedantry) but they also emphasise heavily how polemical the following tales will be. No longer will these writings provide an innocent rendition of experience; on the contrary, they should burn with reformist zeal.

Significant though these textual changes are, they would not be quite so crucial if they did not illustrate how difficult (and therefore how suggestive) a reading of *Gulliver* can be. By 1735, the book had earned popular and courtly plaudits, and Lemuel Gulliver was as much a myth as a literary joke. As with much of his work Swift's name did not appear in the negotiations with publishers. Benjamin Motte, the eventual printer and bookseller, was sent a letter dated 8 August 1726 signed by a Richard Sympson which introduced an abridged *Gulliver* for his professional consideration. The complaints of the 1735 editions about editorial incompetence show a newly irascible side to Gulliver but they are very much a consequence of Swift-as-Gulliver's own secrecy where even the actual abridgement given to Motte was not in Swift's handwriting.[1] This could be due to the fact that 'Gulliver' had not only written a popular classic but a politically dangerous work as well. Even the 1735 edition did not carry the thinly disguised allegory of the Lindalinian (Irish) rebellion which was to have appeared in Book III, Chapter 3.[2] Swift, however, was not slow in making a virtue out of this necessity. Angus Ross' verdict stresses that, whilst an 'important layer of political material' was doubtless the 'centre of editorial disturbance', the prefatory 'mystification' was also an 'important rhetorical device' which placed on the reader 'a burden of active discrimination, and the necessity of exercising caution in interpretation'.[3]

This extends from noting the glaring mistake in the 'Advertisement' where Sympson is described as writing the letter to Gulliver and not vice versa, to becoming uneasy, to say the least, at Gulliver's high-handed Houynhnm certainties and his naive confidence in expecting 'a full stop put to all Abuses and Corruptions' on the strength of this book alone (XI: 6). The interpretative caution noted by Ross is moreover not just a withholding of full assent to Swift's thesis until all is finally revealed, but also a mode of reading in itself. Take Gulliver's closing paragraphs in the letter to Sympson. Initially, we, as 'miserable Animals', observe the mortal sin of Pride personified in Gulliver's inhuman alienation. Alternatively, Gulliver's desire to 'remove that infernal Habit of lying, Shuffling, Deceiving, and Equivocating, so deeply rooted in the very Souls of all my Species; especially the *Europeans*' is surely a very laudable aim, one not so easily dismissed because we have judged his character by our own fallen and mortal norms of conduct. Most certainly Gulliver's predicament is one of a divided identity, for whilst aspiring to Houynhnm perfection, he now feels 'some corruptions of [his] *Yahoo* nature' revive in him through human society, especially of a domestic nature, 'else I should never have attempted so absurd a Project as that of reforming the *Yahoo* Race in this Kingdom; but, I have now done with all such visionary Schemes for ever' (XI: 8). It must be remembered that the Modest Proposer of 1729 was similarly 'wearied out ... with offering vain, idle, visionary Thoughts' of Irish self-help, a passage which parallels Swift's own writing career (XII: 117).

All reading demands initially some measure of trust that the writer is serious in his intentions. Ironic texts often subvert such trust and resist a clear identification of generic rules. *Gulliver* is a spoof travel-book, but its range is broader than in purely literary satire. Travel broadens the mind and also extends our sympathies. In Gulliver's case this is carried to extremes, for he not only changes his skies but also, in a radical and rather unpalatable way, his very self. In both William Dampier's *A Voyage to New Holland* (1703) and Defoe's *Robinson Crusoe* (1719) travellers may undergo stresses and strain, but these bouts of oppression only redouble the will to survive intact and return home. Gulliver however is deeply affected by the alien cultures he encounters to the point where all is cast in doubt, and, through this spectacle, the identities and meanings we habitually find in the writing of all narratives are questioned. Unlike Crusoe's island near Trinidad or Dampier's New Holland, Lilliput cannot exist.[4] Our identification with Gulliver in his adventuring is very much in the travel-book tradition. Remove any possibility of following Gulliver's voyage on the map, however, and the problem of how to take not only Gulliver but also the significance of his tall tales becomes pressing. Conversely, this very strategy helps one cast a colder eye on the apparent transparency of Defoe's plain style and its pretensions to factual reportage.

Defoe and Dampier (amongst many others) portray their protagonists in action that takes place in a recognisable world needing no special effort of assent or denial. *Gulliver* strikes at the very root of all such hypotheses, for it provides a salutary reminder that realism is, after all, conventional and that first-person narrators are not reliable authorities.

Educating Gulliver

There is little doubt that *Gulliver* was both popular and controversial for its first readers. John Arbuthnot informed Swift on 5 November 1726, barely a week after its publication, that '*Gulliver* is in every body's Hands' (CH, p. 61) and John Gay by 17 November observed that 'from the highest to the lowest it is universally read, from the Cabinet-Council to the Nursery'. Interspersed among these very favourable accounts, from fellow Scriblerians, there is much evidence that the satire was keenly felt. Alexander Pope admitted that there were some who thought it 'rather too bold, and too general a Satire' and John Gay felt that 'the Politicians' found the 'Satire on general societies of men ... too severe'. Church-going 'Lady-critics' apparently felt Swift's 'design' was 'impious' and 'an insult on Providence' by its depreciation of 'the works of the Creator' (CH, 62–3). Gulliver's revelations seemed fascinating in their repulsiveness and, in these instances, were taken to be critical of human nature in general. So spotless do the Houynhynms appear that Gulliver, never mind the Yahoos, appears tainted and immediately debased.

This defensive reading of *Gulliver* depends for its outrage on identifying with Gulliver in Book IV, especially when he is patronised by his Houynhynm master and, eventually, when banished from Houynhynm society. One of the most common examination questions on *Gulliver*, however, allows the examinee to advance a different reading. The question runs along the lines of 'Gulliver is not Swift. Discuss' or, in more sophisticated guise, 'Swift is rarely consistent in his endorsement or disapproval of Gulliver. Illustrate', and only the thinnest answer would hold to the view that the human condition is *consistently* represented by Gulliver. His story purports to be a traveller's tale, a tour through 'Several Remote Nations of the World' to provide the reader with vicarious pleasure and perhaps some easily assimilable examples for his/her moral improvement. The net effect of Swift's *Gulliver* is far less easily determined. The novel is far more resonant that its hero's own account—to the point where Gulliver's character and the various perspectives on it we are encouraged to share need, even invite, interpretation. In the edition from 1735 onwards we are prepared for the disintegration of Gulliver's faith in human rationality and compassion. The earlier editions, before the popular myth-making and Gulliver's 'Letter', allow this consternation full effect.

First, Gulliver encounters beings of such diminutive size (the Lilliputians) that we cannot take their pretensions to dignity seriously. Human airs and graces are viewed by Gulliver as the projection of physically insignificant beings so that we deride by association their pomposity in both ethical and intellectual matters. Gulliver, because he is awarded such physical superiority, serves Swift's satire of courts and human pride. He is not, however, resistant enough to avoid imitating some of the factitious grandeur that surrounds him, such as preening himself on the award of the title of Nardac and wishing to clear his name of any adulterous intent concerning the Treasurer's wife—who is six inches high (XI: 65–6).

In Brobdingnag Gulliver suffers as a midget amongst beings who are both exploitative (Glumdalclitch's father) and physically repellent (the Beggars [XI: 112–13] and

61

Maids of Honour [XI: 119] but who also have advantages Gulliver enjoyed previously, of enlarged moral vision. Gulliver's oration before the King is a measure of how Lilliputian he has become. When the King concludes that the 'Bulk' of us must be 'the most pernicious Race of little odious Vermin that Nature ever suffered to crawl upon the Surface of the Earth' (XI: 132), we no doubt feel a common humanity (and shock) with Gulliver. This bond holds throughout much of Book III. On the island of Laputa and at the Academy of Lagado, Gulliver is a constant reminder of humane norms of behaviour confronted by Academicians who propose to extract sub-beams out of cucumbers or so develop 'speculative knowledge by practical and mechanical Operations' that books can be written 'without the least Assistance from Genius or Study' (XI: 183–4). There are also Laputians, who can only be diverted from intense speculations by Flappers who tap their masters to tell them when to speak or listen. Gulliver is by no means a consistently reliable narrator. For example, his capture of the Blefuscudian fleet involves the haulage of 50 men-of-war, each probably 9 feet long, and 'with great Ease' (XI: 52). He may regret his fond visions of the Court during his first voyage, feel suitably downcast after his audience with the Brobdingnagian monarch and grow 'heartily ashamed of the pleasing Visions' he had formed of immortality before meeting the Struldbruggs (XI: 214), but, in so doing, it seems that he is at least capable of some self-questioning.

One of the most obvious problems with Book IV is that such an education, received by learning from experience, is so radically unpleasant. Whereas previously our reading has accepted the possibility that Gulliver is Swift's plaything and that our identification with him is open to endorsements and reversals, the conclusion to the travels is surprisingly inconclusive. Both Dampier and Defoe return to the *terra firma* of social intercourse enriched both materially and ethically by the experience. Gulliver cannot be assimilated in such a way. 'Revived by the Smell' of his stable and conversing with his horses four hours every day (XI: 290), he both resists our sympathy and our approbation. His ludicrousness does not lessen his power to disturb. Indeed, the instinct to dismiss Gulliver as a melancholic misogynist resembles a brittle defensiveness that resists all radical interrogation of the normal conduct of life. The latter is surely awakened when we read past the stable scene of. Chapter 11. In chapter 12 this chastened, 'educated' Gulliver is allowed a less fixated rhetoric with which to address us. No longer can we hold his condition quite so safely at arm's length. It is this chapter, perhaps even more than the preceding ones in the book, that is truly disturbing, in that it seeks to convince us, without neurosis, that Gulliver's vision is not negligible and, what is more, mirrors *Swift's* sentiments accurately.

In the 'Preface of the Author' to *The Battel of the Books*, satire is imaged as 'a sort of *Glass*, wherein Beholders do generally discover every body's Face but their Own; which is the chief Reason for that kind of Reception it meets in the World, and that so very few are offended with it' (I: 140). In more humourous vein, the 'Preface' to the *Tale* finds satiric denunciation of a general nature merely 'a *Ball* bandied to and fro, and every Man carries a *Racket* about Him to strike it from himself among the rest of the Company'. Because this satire was 'levelled at all' each individual 'makes bold to understand it of others, and very wisely removes his particular Part of the Burthen upon the shoulders of the World, which are broad enough, and able to bear it' (I: 31). The *Tale*, as we have seen, penetrates this self-excusing defence by offering no safety for a 'normal' mode of reading. The Teller can still utter true words in jest, whilst remaining a manifestly bad writer, both aesthetically and morally. In Gulliver's case, the crux in our interpretation of the whole text of the *Travels* occurs when we try to comprehend his character—not the style of his writing (which is clear enough) or his narrative (which offers no conflicting points of view or sub-plots). What Swift accomplishes in *Gulliver* is nothing less than a radical reassessment of humane norms through the constant reminder that what we 'know' of Gulliver is only his *written* testimony and, further, what we read may be playful, contradictory and delusive rather than factual, consistent and ethical.

In reviewing the extensive range of *Gulliver* criticism one is often struck by the persistence of interpretations constructed on the coherence model, that is, readings that set out to discover some central (and stable) intention taken to underlie all the surface textual effects. Gulliver is *either* mad and pathetic *or* a soothsayer. If we stress the satiric edge to the first three Books then one is likely to find in Gulliver's tragic alienation Swift's view of the fallen human condition. Alternatively, if the result of the satire is comic (see the rope-dancing episode in Lilliput [XI: 38–9], or Gulliver's music before the Brobdingnagian Court [XI: 126–7]), then Gulliver is no seer and is himself insanely proud. James L. Clifford has termed these two possible conclusions 'hard' and 'soft' options: 'By "hard" I mean an interpretation which stresses the shock and difficulty of the work, with almost tragic overtones, while by "soft", I mean the tendency to find comic passages and compromise solutions.'[5] *Gulliver* supplies both experiences, either intentionally or not. Indeed, if one criticises *Gulliver* textually, then it is quite possible to find in such mutually exclusive options, the contradictoriness and fascination of what is difficult about the work. Far from choosing between the 'hard' and the 'soft' to reproduce what Swift had in mind and so how he designed *Gulliver*, a 'textual' critic is more receptive to the *simultaneity* of such tragi-comedy and how any metaphor will eventually defeat the attempt to explain and so simplify it. What the conclusion to *Gulliver* throws into sharp relief is that the *ethos* of not only Gulliver relating his travels but also Swift in writing Gulliver into existence in the first place is split and flawed, not seamless and direct. The expression, thankfully, always seems to resist, even obstruct, the deducible 'content' taken to be prior to it.

Characterising Gulliver and his 'Travels'

The opening paragraph of Chapter 1 take pains to supply a context for Gulliver, an identifiable 'world' analogous to that experienced by the reader. There are no striking words or arresting phrases, no purple patches of rhetoric or redundant epithets which may detain us on our even paced passage through the narrative. The name, James Bates, carries no hint of caricature, London can be traced on the map and the timespans noted ('Fourteen years old', 'three years' and 'four years') are not symbolic. The mode is realistic in that the writing displays a desire to provide some measure of verisimilitude; events are described that are not obviously literary ones alone. The details can still be interpreted as tendentious, however. W. A. Speck remarks on how Gulliver's earliest training is hardly a normal one for the high seas. Instead of a practical maritime education, his expertise is analytical and rational. His education is, on the other hand, quite consonant with Whiggism and Noncon-formity (Cambridge, Puritan Emmanuel College, Dissenting Leyden). This is made clearer by the 'solid city addresses' to which he returns (Old Jury, Fetter Lane) and his marriage to the daughter of a Newgate Street hosier. Gulliver, therefore, helps Swift endorse a Country Tory ideology by, first, being employed as a 'Whig foil, to satirise the values of the Court Whigs'. Whilst starting out with a naive loyalty to his country's judicature and courtly rituals, Gulliver becomes rapidly disillusioned and ends up 'vehemently rejecting the values of the Court Whigs, including their commitments to commercial expansion and the ascendancy of the Whig oligarchy'.[6] Swift's anti-urban animus and his firm desire for a rooted traditionalism, the Country alternative to City growth and transformation, finds an apt image in a Whig Gulliver exposing his naive lack of common sense and faith in inherited knowledge whilst travelling (continually) away from home, Swift and family. As Frederick Keener illustrates, this *Wanderlust* is most remarkable when it is remembered that, unlike the case of Robinson Crusoe, it does not seem at all necessary (bearing in mind the Nottinghamshire estate) to undergo such hazards in the first place and at the hands of Fortune, a far less reputable guardian than Providence (pp. 98–103). By the opening paragraph of Book II, Gulliver feels that he has been 'condemned by Nature and Fortune to an active and restless life' (XI: 83). By the end of the Book Gulliver is able to identify this incessant activity as his 'evil Destiny' (XI: 149). When setting out in Book III, the 'Thirst' he has for 'seeing the World' continues 'as violent as ever' (XI: 153–4). By Book IV, Gulliver after the 'very happy Condition' of connubial bliss for five months, is all set to alter it, a pregnant wife notwithstanding. 'If [he] could have learned the lesson of knowing when [he] was well', the voyage would not have been attempted (XI: 221). The perils of the travels seem wilfully entertained.

This 'mimetic' explanation for Swift's choice of form finds in the metaphor of travelling a conservative distrust of social as well as physical mobility. Gulliver would have led a well-adjusted life if he had tended his own acres and acknowledged his place in the order of things. His fate is disaffection from all social ritual, retired to his 'little Garden at *Redriff*' where he applies 'those excellent Lessons of Virtue which [he] learned among the *Houynhynms*'. Such isolation from courts and human society on the other hand is hardly exemplary, for the sentence continues that he will 'instruct the Yahoos of [his] own Family as far as I shall find them docible Animals; ... behold my Figure often in a Glass, and thus if possible habituate my self by Time to tolerate the Sight of a human creature' (XI: 295). This proud isolation even entails the blasphemy of denying communion (domestic and perhaps religious) with his own kith and kind (XI: 289–90). This train of political analogising obviously breaks down. Swift's Country Toryism expresses itself in wider terms than in a political allegory, where each satirical signifier has a particular (political) signified.[7] Gulliver's character seems split: one part human and one part a coolly detached observer of his 'Figure' in the glass, or, from another perspective, one part moral reformer, the other disdainful hermit. There seems much more at stake here than the scoring of debating points. If, as F. P. Lock concludes, Swift's indirect methods of narrative were prompted by rhetorical and aesthetic design rather than legal motives (1980, pp. 89–122), then we need to emphasise in our reading the moments when the writing exceeds an initial allegorical or allusive framework. Country Toryism provides no safety as it can hardly approximate to the stoical rationality of the Houynhynms. Indeed, to claim that the whole text is the sum of its local allegories does much to diminish its impact and helps cultivate a selective blindness to the concluding chapters.[8] Lock's point that 'contemporary politics should be thought of as illustrating Swift's points rather than explaining them' (1980, p. 89), need not, however, mean that the 'textual' approach supplies a privileged mode of analysis, freed from the need to provide historical interpretation. On the contrary, it obliges us to try a more sophisticated 'mimetic' approach so as to identify the elements that prompted Swift to construct such paradoxes.

If, as I have suggested, Gulliver enjoys no 'authentic' independence from what we take to be Swift's polemical intention, does this mean that, like Robinson Crusoe or Fielding's Tom Jones, his psychology is only sketched in lightly to lend greater prominence to the broad outlines of the plot? So sophisticated have our expectations become of psychological complexity in novelistic characters that readers reared on high realism are often disappointed if they feel unable to identify with them. When plot determines characters in a novel this would seem to deny such attachment for it is surely easier to appreciate a 'person' than a conceptual framework. In *Gulliver's* case, however, the narrator and hero are one. Plot and its *dramatis personae* both issue from the same source. Consequently, one of the most basic factors in appreciating how *Swift's* text operates is how we react to Gulliver's *ethos*. For Martin Price, Gulliver 'embodies the incorrigible tendency of the mind to oversimplify experience, a trait that takes, with equal ease, the form of complacency or of misanthropy' (1964, pp. 197–8). For us to recognise this, we must also be conscious of some norm that Gulliver transgresses. This sceptical form of reading, judicial rather then empathic is very much nearer to Swift's contempories' own. Ethical concerns (noted above) contributed more directly to matters of satiric taste.

What has also changed since 1726 is the meaning now habitually given to a fictional 'character'. The unconscious, *pace* Freud, is often deemed the prime cause of human behaviour. The depiction of inner deliberation and motivation is very much what the novel form finds most congenial. Dialogue uncovers the public world of social interaction whilst the continuous prose narrative gives the reader access to hidden human desires. Dislocation is evident and often motors the plot. For Swift human 'personality' was not as personal a possession of each individual. Dislocation can happen in the human ego without recourse to more modern marginalising terms from psychiatry such as schizophrenia or paranoia. The individual gained an identity from many perhaps heterogeneous influences.

In psychological studies after John Locke's *Essay*, experience was disturbingly paramount in the formation of character. Man acquires knowledge initially from the 'simple' ideas of sensation derived from the senses. One's 'complex ideas'—ideas of reflection, which are derived from introspection (such as thinking, believing and willing)—are constructed on this 'simple' foundation. 'Primary qualities' of objects are found in all objects such as solidity, its dimensions and mobility; but 'secondary qualities' are nothing but the objects' capacity to produce in us ideas not directly connected with their origin, such as colour, taste and smell. Locke's account, therefore, denied the existence of innate ideas, and thus cast doubt on the stability and durability of 'character' and its individual identity. External physical reality eventually provides all our conceptions. Hobbes had stressed the physical immediacy of this foundation:

> there is no conception in a mans mind, which hath not at first, totally, or by parts, been begotten upon the organs of Sense ... The cause of Sense, is the Externall Body, or Object, which presseth the organ proper to each Sense, either immediatly, as in the Tast and Touch; or mediately, as in Seeing, Hearing, and Smelling. (Part I, Ch. 1, p. 85)

Locke almost delights in the basic foundations he proposes for all subsequent ideals or beliefs. The 'ground-work' for notions about the world derive from 'sense' or one's 'reflection' on 'sense'. 'All those sublime thoughts, which tower above the clouds and reach as high as heaven itself, take their rise and footing here' (II, xxiv, vol. 1, p. 89). As Christopher Fox notes, the concept of a 'substantial self' is a basic necessity for human moral accountability. What Locke replaces it with is selfhood based on *consciousness* not *substance*.[9] If one's 'soul' can be linked mercurially to changes in physical phenomena and so is never quite distinct from one's particular train of experiences, how can the individual be fully responsible both for his/her vices or virtues? 'Character' could be invoked as a vivid and decisively irreducible unit against such intimations of flux and decay.

Literary characterisation, on the other hand, had persistently taken as its model a generalised account of the differences between individuals based on the 'humours' or 'ruling passions' most central to each fictional persona, and therefore most easily explicable in terms of stock motives and traditional types of character. From antiquity their most available catalogue was the *Characters* of Theophrastus. Abel Boyer had recently transplanted them in 1702 (*The English Theophrastus*) and applied them to contemporary English life. In Eustace Budgell's more literal translation, *The Moral Characters of Theophrastus* (1714), the 'Dedication' expresses the older and more coherent doctrine of representation Theophrastus provided: 'It is observed of his Characters, that they are all Simple and Uniform. He has represented a Person in all his Actions, as under the Influence of one particular Disposition of Mind' (sig. A4). However, one page later, Budgell admits that modern life has introduced hybrids inconceivable then, where the same person could be 'Master of all the finer Parts of Learning' as well as being conversant with 'the Intricacies of Commerce, the Springs of publick Credit, and the Interest of his Country' (sig. A5). In 1688 Jean de la Bruyère, in his *Les Caractères*, had provided witty French counterparts to such apparently stolid consistency. In the anonymous translation, *The Characters or the Manners of the Age* (1699), Theophrastus and the Humours psychologists are roundly refuted as *passé* and rather plodding. In the chapter 'Of Men—Their Nature', social complexity visits various identities on social animals, wherein 'the Cares of Life' or 'the Situation they find themselves in and the Law of Necessity' so 'force Nature and cause such great Changes' that a man 'can't tell what to make of himself, his Outside changes so often; has so many Alterations and Revolutions, that he is really neither what he thinks he is himself, nor what he appears to be' (p. 256). La Bruyère not only doubts the powers of accurate introspection but even the possibility of an exact judgement on one's fellows: 'Men have no certain Characters; or if they have any, 'tis that they have none which they always pursue, which never change, and by which they may be known' (p. 297). It is not therefore the case that it was Locke alone who discredited the traditions of predictable character-sketches, for there was French wit as well as English empiricism in the case.

Gulliver's geographical mobility is congruent with his own almost cypher-like mutability. A new land confronts Gulliver with new challenges to his already frail individuality. Each voyage means Gulliver has once again to examine how trustworthy his inherited guides for conduct are. All his preparations for travel, those 'Hours of Leisure ... spent in reading the best Authors, ancient and modern; being always provided with a good Number of Books', involve theory, not practice, and yet, by possessing a good memory, he is capable of learning foreign languages and 'observing the Manners and Dispositions of the People' (XI: 20). Such a facility for mimickry and book-learning discloses a passive understanding, ready to accept what others provide. What remains dangerously untutored is the will and a vigorous moral independence.

Gulliver's 'Truth' is rarely a moral quality. Frequently, he will assure us of his veracity but this is usually in relation to the details of his narrative and not to any universal grasp of

71

ethical problems. He does not refrain from including examples of micturation (such as extinguishing the fire at the Lilliputian Empress' apartment [XI: 56] or even defecation [XI: 29]). Yet, especially in Lilliput, he often suggests a reality exterior to his own abbreviated discourse, not troubling the reader with the minutiae of superfluous description (XI: 74, 76, 79). In Brobdingnag, where the physical threat is more immediate, he rarely spends as much time on providing plausible credentials for his own narrative.

There is one passage, however, where Gulliver begs the 'gentle Reader' for forbearance and, in so doing, suggests a change in tone. After Gulliver's frantic and almost heroic struggle with the monstrous rats on his mistress' bed, an unusually limpid narration of actions rather than state of mind or observations on alien cultures, he apologises for dwelling on his discharging of 'the Necessities of Nature' after it. However, the preceding narrative has surely undercut such precious solicitude for the reader. Gulliver-as-actor has surely excused any unartful story-telling by Gulliver-as-teller. To protest this much is fatuous and, what is more, alerts the reader to the weak sides in his text, especially as to its usefulness. The 'Necessities of Nature' are described, 'however insignificant they may appear to grovelling vulgar Minds', in order to allow philosophers to 'enlarge [their] Thoughts and Imagination, and apply them to the Benefit of publick as well as private Life'. The opposite is truer to the experience of reading *Gulliver*, for such redundancy of detail has no such expansive effect. Gulliver, 'chiefly studious of Truth', cannot deduce from his own experiences any 'complex ideas' of either ethical or aesthetic value. His claim to dispense with 'any Ornaments of Learning, or of Style' promise almost total recall, deflected by the minimum of artifice. Indeed, the sojourn in Brobdingnag 'made so strong an Impression on [his] Mind, and is so deeply fixed in [his] Memory, that in Committing it to Paper, [he] did not omit one material Circumstance'. The very next sentence erases this faithfulness to experience completely: 'However, upon a strict Review, I blotted out several Passages of less Moment which were in my first Copy, for fear of being censured as tedious and trifling, whereof Travellers are often, perhaps not without Justice, accused' (XI: 94). Gulliver is, after all, an artist. The reader cannot receive the unvarnished 'truth' of his first draft at all. We acknowledge the same sense of erasure if we turn to the Prefaces of *Robinson Crusoe* or *Moll Flanders* (1722) after reading the main text. For *Crusoe* we discover that the aim of the whole has not been to mirror the serendipitous events of his travels but 'to justify and honour the Wisdom of Providence in all the Variety of our Circumstances, let them happen how they will'. Whilst there is no 'Appearance of Fiction' in the tale and it provides 'a just History of Fact', this is in turn affirmed by the 'Editor' (p. 1). Moll does not write her own preface either, but rather her amanuensis who has 'put it into a dress fit to be seen, and to make it speak language fit to be read'—not the accents of Newgate prison (p. 28).

'Truth' is therefore a carefully cultivated quality. Gulliver not only cannot often see the wood for the trees but also sometimes selects the wrong trees. His lack of polished story-telling is a process not of innocently delivering what experience has thrust in his way, but of premeditation. He did after all seek out adventures by travelling in the first place. Furthermore, his tales, despite his rather forensic style, are sometimes either openly cosmetic, as in his review of European life for the Brobdingnagian King (XI: 127–32), or downright whimsy, as in his daily fictions or 'ridiculous' stories to amuse the court (XI: 124). The 'Tongue of *Demosthenes* or *Cicero*' that Gulliver invokes to aid him in his celebration of European life, 'in a Style equal to its Merits and Felicity', is exposed as one of the false arts of rhetoric (XI: 127). Style has obscured the truth not uncovered it. Indeed, when Gulliver declares that 'nothing but an extreme Love of Truth' led him to disclose such observations critical of European Life (XI: 133), the net effect is to increase the force of such criticisms—an indictment which undermines Gulliver's own privileged European perspective. Immediately there follows his wrong-headed account of the discovery and use of gunpowder which only demonstrates his own '*narrow Principles* and *short Views*' not the King's (XI: 135).

In the first two Books these mystifying devices divide the meaning of what Gulliver tells us from the *significance* we give it in our reading. Whilst we may be enmeshed in Gulliver's rhetoric and perceive a difference between author and fictional character, most readings find it particularly difficult to cut their way out of its snares because our appreciation of what *Swift* intends is just not sharp enough. Claude Rawson's observation on *Gulliver* and Swift's work in general, that its 'bewildering uncertainty' of genre is really a form of 'authorial aggression' (1973, p. 5) goes some way towards defining such indirection. Swift, in a letter to Pope (29 September 1725) claimed that it was the 'Chief End' in all of his endeavours 'to vex the World rather than divert it' (*Corr* 3: 102). Much of this vexation lies in the defiantly 'open' interpretations we are forced to countenance. Gulliver's 'Truth' ignores the wider human propositions that guide all social conduct and, in being so very receptive to his experiences, he loses some of his identity. On the other hand, this is far from providing a conservative endorsement of his own selfhood and the culture he sporadically represents. It is not just that Gulliver is a rather naive and fallible narrator but rather that he is *too* truthful to allow us to take his conventional pieties on trust. A more quiescent, 'European' account would surely have toned down the Brobdingnagian monarch's disgust, or the absurd 'lenity' of the Lilliputian impeachment articles (XI: 68–74). When Gulliver addresses us directly or when he is particularly aware of the need to convince us of his veracity by rhetorical means, Swift invariably denies him full readerly assent. When, however, Gulliver's narrative describes his *actions* or the alien cultures he meets, the narrative style is virtually 'unliterary' and colourless—more realistic and therefore more trustworthy.

Defining and Describing

Just like those Lilliputians charged with providing an inventory of the objects in Gulliver's possession, reading each travel is a process of cautious discovery. The first item is recorded for us in Lilliputian terms: 'IMPRIMIS, In the right Coat-Pocket of the *Great Man Mountain* (for so I interpret the Words *Quinbus Flestrin*) after the strictest Search, we found only one great Piece of coarse Cloth, large enough to be a Foot-Cloth for your majesty's chief Room of State' (XI: 34). The description may be of a handkerchief but it is only apprehensible to the searchers as a state carpet. Similarly, Gulliver is mountainous but, before we can be sure of even that, translation has had to occur. Gulliver is literally a '*Quinbus Flestrin*' for Lilliputians. To understand another culture is a feat of analogical ingenuity. Analogies do, however, break down at some point.

In the last section I argued that Gulliver's own power to understand both the Lilliputians and Brobdingnagians depended on a criterion of 'Truth' often rendered inadequate by a context that eluded the enumeration of facts and accurate observation. For both Dampier and Defoe travelling brought the foreign or alien securely within our ken. Dampier quite literally maps the lands he explores and records events all eventually subservient to an autobiographical framework. Everett Zimmerman notes that the patterns later in the text show Dampier's apparent factuality giving way to the conventions of spiritual autobiography (pp. 135-6). In dedicating his *New Voyage* to Charles Montagu, the President of the Royal Society, Dampier wished to pass off his *experiences* as *fact*. Earlier explorers of the Renaissance had felt their travel was a training for either public life or aesthetic enrichment. The Royal Society viewed their role as quite different. Between January 1665 and March 1667, the first two years of publication, the *Philosophical Transactions* contained twelve models for research when travelling.[10] Observation of alien cultures led naturally to classification, whether of native flora or human traditions. Swift recognised Dampier as Gulliver's guiding light in his letter to Sympson of 1735 where Dampier is supposed to have had his style corrected in the *New Voyage* and his writings 'put ... in Order' (by students) due to Gulliver's advice (XI: 5). For Dampier, as for the early Gulliver, this cultural imperialism is blind to all those elements that cannot fit the Natural History paradigm, and impervious to the radical education earlier travellers expected.

By 1719 and Defoe's *Crusoe*, this philosophical positivism was deployed as a powerful aid to the conventions of realism, namely redundant, non-metaphorical details, reliable narration and generalisation deduced from the apparently unfiltered account of events. Lennard J. Davis has recently claimed that such realism's guarantees of 'truth' derived directly from a shift from romance conventions in prose narratives to those of journalism (the 'News/Novels discourse'). In Defoe's case, 'fact was just another form of fiction and fiction was just a particular category of fact' (p. 173). Indeed, *Crusoe* attracted very little critical comment on its fictional merits until Rousseau's praise in 1762 (*Emile*; *CH*, pp. 52-3) and James Beattie's distinction between the religious and moral allegory of Bunyan's *Pilgrim's Progress* and *Gulliver*, and the serious romance which includes *Crusoe* ('On

Fable and Romance' [1783]; CH, pp. 59–60). Crusoe not only makes his island over to himself ideologically, but also materially too. His labour constructs a life that is recognisable and familiar. He constructs a spade out of ironwood, makes a calendar from a post, bakes his own bread, constructs a canoe and most effectively 'civilises' his Man Friday, teaching him to speak English, shoot and wear clothes. Here is no passive cataloguing, but a determined attempt to maintain one's selfhood in the face of desolating solitude. Crusoe is not unchanged by the whole experience (he undergoes a religious conversion and begins to recognise the 'Voice of Providence' [pp. 91–4]), but his identity, like Dampier's, is virtually unchallenged. He may fear for his life but, by dint of inner resources and a sturdy faith, he is triumphant. In both *A New Voyage* and *Crusoe* there are undeniably traces of the genre of spiritual autobiography which provide an account of spiritual change. Neither of the two protagonists, however, question their own veracity of perspective and narration or, indeed, have it questioned.

In the early development of the modern novel form the factually fictional and the fictionally presented moral fable share several characteristics. Readerly assumptions were also fluid and unformed. *Crusoe*, in one of the very few early critical comments, could be taken to task for providing no 'useful moral, either expressed or understood' and of being stuffed quite improbably with as many 'Reflections' as would 'swell the Bulk of [the] Treatise up to a five Shilling Book' without any innate 'Variety' deduced from the subject (Charles Gildon, *The Life and Strange Surprizing Adventures of Mr. D... De F...*, *of London, Hosier* ([1719]; CH., pp. 44–6). On the other hand, *Gulliver* could be found wanting for not providing a plausible rationality. Jonathan Smedley complained in 1728 that, whereas Defoe's Crusoe had spoken 'in Nature, and by the Novelty of the Adventures, reasonably excited the Reader's Curiosity', Swift provides the very wildest of romantic fantasies:

> Cruso, does nothing but what might be done by a rational
> Creature in the like Circumstances: Gulliver goes mad after
> Fairies, Giants, Horses; and gets nothing Abroad but a mortal
> Hatred to his wedded Wife, whom he leaves, in Breach of his
> matrimonial Vow, and runs away with a Mare. ([Swift] CH, p.
> 91)

Gildon had expected a moral allegory whereas Smedley
distrusted Swift's appropriation of the travel-book form for a
Utopian fantasy.

This generic clash provokes more than a misreading of
Gulliver. The opposed readings of a Utopian account and a
circumstantial and exact Natural History are part of a basic
dichotomy. What appears to be a factual account, providing
useful knowledge of natural phenomena, becomes shot
through with traces of a more satirical mode. This becomes
obvious in several episodes. Gulliver's sudden lapse into
nautical jargon during the storm that eventually lands him in
Brobdingnag (XI: 84), the mathematical word diagram
elucidating the motion of Laputa (XI: 168-9), and the visit to
the Lagadian academy's 'Universal Artist' (XI: 182-6) all
isolate the word as object solely. The mathematical certainty
promised by the Royal Society is never accurate in its
depiction of alien cultures in Gulliver or even of mapping
reality accurately. Sea terms indicate such particularised
objects and actions that communication is blurred.[11] Laputa
moves very simply and should therefore be described in plain
terms. The ingenious Lilliputians are diligence itself in
designing clothes for their gigantic visitor, yet Gulliver
reminds us, 'Nature' had 'adapted the Eyes of the Lilliputians
to all Objects proper for their View: They see with great
Exactness, but at no great Distance' (XI: 57). The
Brobdingnagians cannot conceive of Gulliver's distress,
whereas the Laputians are so speculative that their women are

unfaithful (XI: 165–6) and their schemes leave their colony, Balnibarbi, desperately impoverished (XI: 174–8). Throughout *Gulliver* parables of incomprehension and partial vision abound which stretch language's power to understand the unknown to the limit and beyond.

As Timothy Reiss demonstrates, the 'Euclidean' projects of the Royal Society cut against the grain of such perceptual relativity. In aspiring to inaugurate a method leading to just one right order of perception, Science reproduces 'the facts *before* they are intellectually "constructed" ' and lays claim to a 'common sense' which is the same regardless of perspective: 'the order is "transparent" ' (p. 329). Does this imply, therefore, that Swift believed in the ultimate relativity of all perspectives, or was he fearful of it? When Gulliver is entertained by the Lord Munodi on Balnibarbi, the contrast between his estates and their more scientifically run hinterland is telling. Without, the soil is barren, housing ill-contrived and people in 'Mistery and Want' but, within, all is well regulated, despite his countrymen's ridicule. The Modern is expressed in the Lagadian Academy's authoritarian prescriptions to put all architecture and agriculture 'upon a New Foot'. The Ancient Munodi, however, lacks such 'enterprizing Spirit' and is 'content to go in the old Forms; to live in the Houses his Ancestors had built, and act as they did in every Part of Life without Innovation' (XI: 175–7). Munodi gets his sums right because he is *not* receptive to new experiences and can therefore withstand the influence of ephemeral developments, no matter how popular. Time and tradition not only sanctify belief but also provide a yardstick of inherited wisdom that helps one to identify the traditional mainstream and differentiate it from the eccentric and fixated.

In Reldresal, Glumdalclitch, Munodi and Pedro de Mendez there appear individual models for conduct set against the lemming-like docility of their whole species. This is consistent with a famous letter Swift wrote to Pope whilst revising *Gulliver*, expressing a hatred for 'all Nations professions and Communityes' and a love for 'individualls ... principally I hate and detest that animal called man, although I heartily love John Peter, Thomas and so forth' (*Corr*, 3: 103). The exceptions prove the rule invidious. Ultimately, Gulliver can only interpret phenomena according to probabilities derived from their 'primary qualities'. The leap to the evaluation of such simplicities involves us in a *moral* world. Species are 'natural' and normal; the individual alone can rise above such mass characteristics which are inherited, not achieved. The amoral observations of the Royal Society project involved no element of evaluation— hence Gulliver's intense regard for recording generalities and the belief that this is all there is to be said about their existence. His narrative, however, presents to us *individual* instances or events which do not necessarily tally with the definitions or general tendencies he observes in the species as a whole. Actions will always speak louder in Gulliver's account than his less than authoritative words.

Gulliver-as-narrator and Gulliver-as-actor in his own fiction are at odds. At the conclusion to the text he is unable to conceive of particular people at all, but only 'that animal called man'. When exiled from the Houynhynms, his design is to discover some uninhabited island, free of Yahoos, where he might 'at least enjoy [his] own Thoughts' and reflect on the Houynhynms' example 'without any Opportunity of degenerating into the Vices and Corruptions of [his] own Species'. This reminds him of the ship's mutiny which precipitated the adventure in the first place. Putting into the '*South-East* Point of *New-Holland*', he confronts twenty or so 'Natives' who are 'stark naked', one of whose number attack him by discharging an arrow wounding him 'on the Inside of [his] left knee'—a mark he will carry to his grave. Both physically and psychologically Gulliver is marked by his experience of *typical* behaviour patterns. Paddling back out to sea he shuns Don Pedro's ship and returns to the savages' island rather than trusting himself to '*European Yahoos*' (XI: 283–5). This partial interpretation of experience leaves him totally unfit to receive Pedro de Mendez's civilities with good grace. The individual good man Gulliver cannot exempt from his blanket abhorrence of all humanity, *including himself*. He introduces himself to the Portuguese crew as a 'poor *Yahoo*, banished from the *Houynhynms*' (XI: 285), and yet in conversation with the eminently hospitable Pedro de Mendez, it is the captain who is a Yahoo, and Gulliver who is imbued with Houynhynm superiority. Gulliver's perspectives shift violently. This inevitably challenges the reader to define and describe the *experience* of reading the work, especially when addressed directly in the last chapter by Gulliver-as-narrator.

Abstraction and Context

For the 'textual' critic authorship can be the site of several varied rhetorical functions. Reading is the search for definition and identity, a coming to terms with the contours of narrative. In 'mimetic' terms we can find in Gulliver's alienation a tragic *loss* of identity in his inability to 'read' human behaviour with charity and accuracy. His travelling has led him far from home and left him there. Swift's writing in the last chapter of *Gulliver* provides no goal achieved, in that it provokes more travelling through the significance of the text and does not close down our options—this, despite the hortatory posture of *Gulliver* at the text's conclusion and the opportunities for ethical judgement, such as the excoriation of human pretensions to pride and the alternative of the life of reason. Terry Eagleton recognises that *Gulliver* tempts the reader with the bait of the coherent subject wherein we must either agree or disagree with Gulliver, and search for the likely 'Swift' who directs this psychodrama. Gulliver is however 'traversed and devastated by intolerable contradiction', aspiring to ideal rationality whilst horribly aware of his most basic animality and also wishing for a linguistic materialism (the desire for colourless description) whilst offering himself up to metaphoric restlessness (colourful textuality):

> There is no way for the reader to 'totalise' these contradictions, which the text so adroitly springs upon him; he is merely caught in their dialectical interplay, rendered as eccentric to himself as the lunatic Gulliver, unable to turn to the refuge of an assuring authorial voice. To deconstruct the reader, reducing him from positioned subject to a function of polyphonic discourses: this is the *ideological* intervention accomplished by all of Swift's writing.[12]

Gulliver ultimately discovers very much his own voice or 'character', but characterising *Swift's* text is rendered all but impossible. The 'positioned subject' (first-person narrator and our human representative in alien lands) is unfixed during the narrative until we are confronted by its replacement: a set of 'polyphonic discourses' (simultaneous and irreconcilable significances and styles of writing). Eagleton claims that this forms an '*ideological* intervention', implying that such textual contradictions are somehow willed and a deliberate political strategy. In disputing the reader's commonsense assumptions Swift attempts to have us comprehend Gulliver's chilling discovery that human nature is distasteful yet perhaps our only birthright.

The individual may be able to cultivate some rational and supranatural behaviour but one could not expect more than a handful of humans to manage it. In biographical terms, it is quite possible to find in Gulliver's identification of mankind with the Yahoos or his imprisonment on the sea-shore by

Lilliputian cunning a facet of Swift's hurt pride and political despair. In a letter to Thomas Sheridan, dated 11 September 1725, Swift associates current politics with *Gulliver's* fictional extremes. Complimenting Sheridan on having 'read enough' to acquaint him with the 'nature of man', he takes upon himself the 'character' of a 'discarded courtier' advising a fellow exile to 'sit down and be quiet' and 'expect no more from man than such an animal is capable of'. If this wise retirement is Sheridan's he will 'every day find [his] description of Yahoos more resembling' and so he should 'think and deal with every man as a villain, without calling him so, or flying from him, or valuing him less' (*Corr*, 3: 93–4). The Yahoos resemble the current stars in the political ascendant; the Houynhynms provide an unattainable ideal which, like the simple legislature of the Brobdingnagians, provides a convenient stick to beat the corrupt present. This Old Whiggism or Country Toryism, however, can be found in embryo as early as 1714, a period of relative public prominence for Swift, with the chapter 'Of the secession of Martinus and some hints of his Travels' in *The Memoirs of Martinus Scriblerus* (of composite Scriblerian authorship). In the second voyage Martinus finds himself in 'the Land of the *Giants*, now the most humane people in the world' and in the fourth, he discovers 'a Vein of Melancholy proceeding almost to a Disgust of his Species'. Above all, however, he is heir to 'a mortal Detestation to the whole flagitious Race of *Ministers*' (p. 165). This adversarial ideology endorses the exiled individual ('John, Peter, Thomas and so forth') at the expense of the abstract framework of ministries and percentage probabilities. No doubt this original scheme took on a particular application in the 1720s, but the groundwork for Gulliver's 'melancholy' had already been laid: the vantage-point of the non-aligned satirist. Such alienation is necessary if the closing attack on the reader is to gain *gravitas* and that 'Lump of Deformity, and Diseases both in Body and

Mind, smitten with *Pride*' be contrasted with the eminent rationality of the Houynhynms (XI: 296). It is an open question, however, whether Gulliver as discredited narrator can be considered apart from his closing words, as if such sermons on pride can take on a universal application irrespective of who utters them.

This distrust of inhuman abstraction takes several forms in *Gulliver*. In the visit to the Academy at Lagado those projectors who advance a linguistic materialism turn out to be comically wrong-headed. 'Speculative learning' (the possession of the *'universal Artist'*) (XI: 182), the school of languages who sponsor schemes for excluding verbs and participles from discourse or 'abolishing all Words whatsoever' (XI: 185) and, more insidious, the political interests of the acrostic-hunters and decoders of 'seditious' writing (XI: 190–2)—these are projects which remove language from the persons who use it. Personality is eradicated because it is basically unscientific and anarchic, but Gulliver's own abstract expectations are often proved inadequate (the Struldbruggs, his own confidence in his non-Yahoo nature), and his desire to correct his own mental world in line with his travelling is always questioned (see his returns home).

Gulliver is often more resourceful than the 'hard' interpreters give him credit for. He may *express* self-disgust but his humanity and his *actions* are often saving graces. In Lilliput Gulliver saves the state by his Blesfuscudian raid and also the Empress' apartment from fire. In Brobdingnag, even whilst belittled by the King, Gulliver would be heroic in more auspicious circumstances, for his context, so minutely described, is threatening and so invites a certain defensive empathy. He is buffeted in his box on the journey to the metropolis, has altercations with the gigantic Queen's dwarf, is showered by hailstones the size of tennis-balls and comes near to extinction at the hands of a dog and a monkey. The repulsive proximity of Gulliver's Brobdingnagian experiences provide such a pattern of events as confound paraphrase or abstraction. His courage in the face of such threats, the fight with the wasps (XI: 109–10), the kite (XI: 117) and the stunning of the linnet (XI: 118), not to mention the fight with the rats (XI: 93), is a virtue of activity. When Gulliver reflects on the human condition he is diminished but when he acts instinctively he saves himself.

Whenever Gulliver travels, problems of generic definition are inevitably raised. For example, when Gulliver encounters a Brobdingnagian for the first time, he appears 'as Tall as an ordinary Spire-Steeple' (XI: 86). A Houynhynm is not obviously different from any European horse at first and the Yahoos, far from being a reflection of *human* behaviour, are a convenient alternative of sordid bestiality, a species 'against which [Gulliver] *naturally* conceived' the strongest 'Anti-pathy' (my italics, XI: 224). It is the Houynhynms who see Gulliver as a Yahoo first and it is they who lead him to realise the strength of such an analogy: 'The Beast and I were brought close together,: ... My Horror and Astonishment are not to be described, when I observed, in this abominable Animal, a perfect human Figure.' Only his clothes, 'whereof [the Houynhynms] had no Conception', prevent the similarities of the two figures appearing obvious (XI: 229–30). In the *Tale*, when the beau is stripped in the Teller's presence or when the woman is flayed, it is easy to believe that the 'unsuspected Faults' of natural humanity should remain hidden because of the shocking indecorum of equating skin, an innate covering, with fashionable clothes, the fruit of luxury. The life of the unaccommodated man is only held to be as cheap as a beast's when all the social and so artificial elements of life are discounted. Gulliver is robbed of these stabilising terms of reference by being inserted in non-human societies. Crusoe can create a recognisably regulated habitat for himself but he has no alternative social pattern to confront. 'The Beast' is indeed brought up close to mankind in the opening chapters of the fourth voyage, but only by denying that man's social accoutrements are a sufficient safeguard against Yahoo-like anarchy.

This is tragic news indeed for the 'European' reader. However, such 'hard' reflections are abstract criticisms of the human genus, blind to its particular instances. Gulliver does not go under in either Brobdingnag or Houynhynmland. When faced with starvation by refusing the Yahoo's 'Ass's Flesh' (XI: 230), he responds resourcefully by 'contriving' a kind of wholemeal bread. Although 'a very insipid Diet', it is 'common enough in many Parts of *Europe*' (perhaps Ireland) and 'grew tolerable by Time; and having been often reduced to hard fare in [his] life' Gulliver realises 'how easily Nature is satisfied' and how healthy such a regimen can prove to be (XI: 232). The detail of this description and that of the canoe he fashions for his departure (XI: 281–2) celebrates Gulliver's industry and robust independence from enervating delicacy. This natural response is not that of the Yahoos or even that of the rational abstraction of the Houynhynms, in that it is a reaction to an adverse context with unforeseen resourcefulness. When returning to familiar social inter-course such flexibility deserts Gulliver. What was once habitual can no longer be trusted or even tolerated. Meanwhile his nose is kept 'well stopt' with 'Rue, Lavender, or Tobacco-Leaves' (XI: 295): a 'hard' interpreter of his own experiences.

Superficially, this realisation on Gulliver's part would seem to be an appreciation of man as part angel and part beast. Presumptuous man conceives himself as purely angelic yet is deluded. Pope's *An Essay on Man* (1733–34) could have been Swift's text:

> Then say not Man's imperfect, Heav'n in fault;
> Say rather, Man's as perfect as he ought;

His knowledge measur'd to his state and place,
His time a moment, and a point his space ...
(*Epistle I*, ll. 69–72, p. 507)

The tutelary spirits of Pope's poem are Order and God's Providence, however various its explorations. In Swift's work however such achieved balance has no obvious place. Gulliver's 'knowledge' cannot be 'measur'd to his state and place' because he no longer knows what these should or could be.

In taking *Gulliver* to be metaphorical play rather than the expression of an individual ego, the 'textual' critic is not as worried about such mimetic problems, because (s)he does not proceed on the assumption that a writer's 'character' can be extrapolated from the text that bears the appropriate signature. Signifying dominates over our power to identify its signifieds with any degree of certainty. The centre can never hold because it is constantly dispersed or absent, never coherent. Swift's narrative displays a particular subject in Gulliver in the act of telling a tale. The reader is always *obliged* to interpret Swift's writing for his 'presence' or meaning. This search for an identity between verbal form and conceptual content, a primary task of all interpretation, is here presented as the type of all narratorial problems: how can any writer be believed if all language is prey to readerly subjectivity?

This anxiety, and its extension into all areas of epistemology, recurs constantly throughout *Gulliver*. The admirable Brobdingnagians are concerned only with 'what may be useful in Life.... And as to Ideas, Entities, Abstractions and Transcendentals, [Gulliver] could never drive the least Conception into their Heads'. Their laws are not susceptible of more than one interpretation and, furthermore, it is even a 'capital Crime' to 'write a Comment' on any aspect of the legal system. Their libraries are small and their style so 'clear, masculine, and smooth' that large tomes would be a clear example of 'Florid' failure (XI: 136-7). His return to human society involves more tale-telling in order that the captain of the rescuing vessel might understand him. 'Truth,' Gulliver believes, 'always forceth its Way into rational Minds.' Consequently, he believes that his 'plain Relation' will pass for fact, however outlandish the events may appear. He is even scornful of travellers' tales in general in that he can only deal in 'little beside common Events', which is not their stock-in-trade. Gulliver may be right but the norms of just what may count as plain and simple do not stand clear of a social context where account needs to be taken of an audience. When the captain suggests that his adventures might make a good book, Gulliver seems innocent of the volume we have in our hands: 'My Answer was, that I thought we were already overstocked with Books of Travels: That nothing could now pass which was not extraordinary;...'. He, on the contrary, could not supply 'ornamental Descriptions of strange Plants, Trees, Birds and other Animals' or the fantastic rites of a 'savage People' (XI: 146-7).

At such moments, Gulliver's own admiration for the straightforwardness of the Brobdingnagians renders him vulnerable to a 'human' reading of his circumstances. Gulliver has certainly *not* provided 'common events' by a 'human' yardstick; neither has he been innocent of embellishing the truth. The desire for a transparent medium of communication is thwarted by the larger designs of the narrative. Instinctively imagining himself still amongst giants, Gulliver greets his family with all the signs of one who has lost his wits. He admits this by describing himself behaving 'unaccountably'. Such is the 'great Power of Habit and Prejudice' (XI: 149). Swift is also not averse to representing the Brodingnagian project of linguistic materialism in a most unflattering light in the Lagadian school of languages. Any project for 'entirely abolishing all Words' and relying on producing the things to which they refer in conversation not only robs humanity of its moral vocabulary but also demonstrates the inadvisability of wrenching words from their most appropriate context: an active communication expressing the self (XI: 185).

The Houynhynms not only have no conception of clothes (XI: 230) but also none of books or literature (XI: 235). Seeing that the 'Use of Speech was to make us understand one another, and to receive Information of Facts', the Houynhynms can regularise their speech in line with the things expressed as if personality and speech can be separated (XI: 240). When Gulliver embraces this impersonal paradigm, dislocation ensues, but for Houynhynms language is itself passionate not just a means of *signifying* passion (XI: 226). It can perform what it wants to express as with the Grey's protection of Gulliver by neighing 'in a Style of Authority' (XI: 228). The Houynhynm brand of perfection lies in their careful management of communication. They can never be traduced by written documents as are the three brothers in the *Tale* for they have no writing and rely on 'traditional' knowledge alone, without any irritable questing after interpretation or modification. Their poetry is transmitted orally and their poets are noted for the 'Justness of their Similes, and the Minuteness, as well as Exactness of their Descriptions' which are 'inimitable' (XI: 273). Such equable rationality cannot be reduced to its first principles in that it is instinctive and so unsystematic. Its uncritical adoption by Gulliver, however, leads only to solitary abstraction. When we encounter the last chapter of the book, therefore, the clash between 'Ornament' and 'Truth' occurs not just in Gulliver's relation but Swift's as well. Gulliver's neurosis may be truth and error may be endemic. Only an immensely proud person can separate him or herself enough from human presumption in order to castigate it.

In 'textual' terms Swift's text displays a yearning for non-verbal truth, the bedrock on which humanity might erect its morality and identify duplicity and corruption. This edifice of divine security and non-figurative stature is, however, founded on standards of linguistic 'purity' that smack of the Royal Society and its travel-book progeny. We can go further than the 'textual' critics on the other hand. Swift had good reason to write as he did in *Gulliver*. In the Stella birthday ode of 1727 Swift finds some consolation for a dying Esther Johnson. Memories of past happiness should be infused with the consciousness of a life spent virtuously: a 'radiant dart/To shine through life's declining part' (ll. 13-4, p. 314). Such acts of kindness must not be said to have disappeared, for 'Does not the body thrive and grow/By food of twenty years ago?' (ll. 55-6). These must not 'like empty shadows pass,/Or forms reflected from a glass' (ll. 51-2, p. 315). The reality of the present is so direct a result of the past that the two coexist, the past traceable in the present, yet, at the same time, Swift could be extremely dubious about the possibility of such self-knowledge. Stella's virtue may only be obvious to another, not to herself.

In a sermon printed with Swift's more authenticated work from 1744 onwards, entitled 'The Difficulty of Knowing One's Self', self-knowledge is a particularly vagrant possession, 'for a Man can no more know his own Heart than he can know his own Face, any other Way than by Reflection' (XI: 355). The opinion of friends and associates may be nearer the truth than one's own opinion. However, reflection (in the sense of contemplation) can provide some measure of assurance, but it is not performed.

> without some Pain and Difficulty: For, before a Man can reflect upon himself, and look into his Heart with a steady Eye, he must contract his Sight, and collect all his scattered and roving Thoughts into some Order and Compass, that he may be able to take a clear and distinct view of them. (IX: 356)

There are no students' guides to these moments of revelation. Individuals can only occasionally and after strenuous self-examination achieve this insight. 'Judge not, that ye be not judged' (Matthew 7:1) and 'God is the Judge: he putteth down one, and setteth up another' (Prayer book 75:7) were common Anglican texts. From these sources Swift derived his scepticism about human character. Its intensity, however, no doubt came from more secular sources. Swift's distaste for Defoe's prose style in the *Review* (1704–14), derived from its 'grave, sententious, dogmatical' rhetoric (*A Letter Concerning the Sacramental Test* [1709], II: 113) and 'mock authoritative Manner' (*Examiner* no. 15, 16 November, 1710, III: 13). Such self-possession Swift found impertinent. When reflecting on himself, Swift wrote coolly. His own *Verses on the Death of Dr. Swift* (1731) are disparaging when his friends and acquaintances are quoted. The truest opinion comes from 'One quite indifferent in the cause' who alone can draw his 'character impartial' (ll.305–6, p. 493) and only well after his death. As Edward Said points out, 'the *Verses* deliver Swift to history at the poem's end' (p. 71), but this impartiality and lasting memorial is expressed only by chance at 'A club assembled at the Rose' and only by *one* of their number.[13]

In *Gulliver*, therefore, the difficulty of knowing not just Gulliver but also Swift himself forms part of a major preoccupation of philosophical writing as well as theological debate. Man must be morally accountable, just as some yardstick be discovered to call political corruption in account as well. When on Glubbdubdrib, Gulliver is permitted to see 'Scenes of Pomp and Magnificence' and allowed to compare the great authors and their commentators' account of them as well as gauge how accurate historians had been in describing the past (XI: 195–202), he uncovers a pattern of misrepresentation and mock-heroism. Interpretation and historiography are part of elaborate whispering-games, the

original context sometimes tantalisingly elusive and sometimes criminally ignored. If it is true that much of character
was judged on its probability,[14] it is also remarkable how
many exceptions there were to this rule at the time. Matthew
Prior, when returning to the skilful ordering imaged by
Edmund Spenser's Alma in the House of Temperance (*Faerie
Queene* [1590–96], Book 2, Canto IX), finds in the
contemporary soul no progressive enlightenment or enduring
consistency. In the third canto of *Alma; or, The Progress of the
Mind* (1718), system-builders are really erecting plausible
frameworks for their own fixations:

> Atoms You cut; and Forms You measure,
> To gratifie your private Pleasure;
> 'Till airy Seeds of casual Wit
> Do some fantastic Birth beget ...
> Caught by your own delusive Art,
> You fancy first, and then assert.
> (ll.29–32, 37–8, I, pp. 500–1)

George Berkeley, a later Trinity College graduate and a friend
of Swift's later years, is often typified as a philosopher of
immaterialism in that he held to the view that objects cannot
be said to exist unperceived by human sense. In Locke's
writings there appeared what seemed to be a commonsense
alternative: *real* 'primary qualities' hooked up to subjective
'secondary' ones. In the 'Introduction' to the *Principles of
Human Knowledge* (1710), on the other hand, Berkeley could
turn the tables, and criticise Locke's belief in such abstract
ideas as the 'primary qualities' of objects. *In fact*, one never
actually perceived a 'primary quality' aside from contingent
'secondary' ones:

> For example, the mind having observed that Peter, James and
> John, resemble each other, in certain common agreements of
> shape and other qualities, leaves out of the complex or

compounded idea it has of Peter, James, and any other particular man, that which is peculiar to each, retaining only what is common to all; and so makes an abstract idea wherein all the particulars equally partake, abstracting entirely from and cutting off all those circumstances and differences, which might determine it to any particular extreme. (p. 67)

In the midst of Locke's 'corpuscularian' view of nature (that objects actually possess such 'primary qualities' independent of any 'secondary' judgement), Berkeley saw the myth of abstraction. Gulliver's Royal Society paper on the 'Remote Nations of the World' attempts an unsparingly 'primary' account yet cannot escape its own context and perspective for the realm of abstraction. Prior's attack on systematising moralists finds comic capital in human mutability. Any reading of *Gulliver* must confront similar comedy as well as its hinterland of inexpressible fear.

Notes

1. For a full account of *Gulliver*'s textual history, see Harold Williams' Introduction to Vol. IX of the *Prose Writings*, pp. xxi–xxviii, and David Woolley's 'Swift's Copy of *Gulliver's Travels*: The Armagh *Gulliver*, Hyde's edition, and Swift's earliest corrections', in Probyn (a), pp. 131–78. The success of *Gulliver* also brought forth a sub-literature of pirated editions and chapbooks (popular adaptations or digests). See Pat Rogers' remarks on *Gulliver*, in Rivers, pp. 41–4.
2. This is reprinted at XI: 309–10. See also the other substantial emendations at XI: 311, 315–17, 318.
3. *Swift: Gulliver's Travels* (London, 1968), p. 19. See also the whole of Ross' succinct account of the writing process at pp. 15–19.
4. I take Lord Scarborough's anecdote (re-told by John Arbuthnot to Swift) concerning 'a Master of a ship, who told him that he was very well acquainted with Gulliver', and Arbuthnot's 'old Gentleman' who, on borrowing *Gulliver*,

went 'immediately to his Map to search for Lillyput' (*CH*, pp. 61-2) as credulous exceptions to a more discriminating rule.

5. 'Gulliver's Fourth Voyage: "Hard" and "Soft" Schools of Interpretation', *Quick Springs of Sense*, ed. Larry S. Champion (Athens, Ga., 1974), pp. 33-49 (p. 33).

6. *Society and Literature in England* 1700-60 (Dublin, 1983), pp. 67-8.

7. It could, however, be read as just political satire. See *A Letter from a Clergyman to his Friend* ... (1726; *CH* pp. 66-70), and Jonathan Smedley's apocryphal 'Fourth Volume' of Pope and Swift's *Miscellanies*, entitled *Gulliveriana* (1728; *CH* pp. 90-2).

8. Lock's plea for a more universal reading of the satire has not gone unchallenged. See J. A. Downie, pp. 274-87, 373. This disagreement is often merely one of emphasis: Downie does not deny that there is greater significance in the satire and Lock does not deny that there is much localised political material. See also W. J. McCormack, 'On *Gulliver's Travels*', *Narrative: From Malory to Motion Pictures*, ed. Jeremy Hawthorn (London, 1985), pp. 76-7.

9. 'Locke and the Scriblerians: The Discussion of Identity in Early Eighteenth-Century England', *Eighteenth-Century Studies*, 16 (1982-83), 1-25. See also Patrick Coleman's 'Character in an Eighteenth-Century Context', *The Eighteenth Century*, 24 (1983), 51-63.

10. These were collected together in 1692 as *General Heads for a Natural History of a Countrey*. For a fuller account see George B. Parks, 'Travel as Education', *The Seventeenth Century: Studies in the History of English Thought and Literature from Bacon to Pope* (Stanford, Ca., 1951), pp. 264-90; and Michael Hunter, *Science and Society in Restoration England* (Cambridge, 1981) pp. 53-4.

11. This is a direct reference to Dampier's retention of some 'sea-terms' because he writes as a seaman, not a professional writer, 'choosing to be more particular than might be needful, with respect to the intelligent Reader' ('Preface', sig. A3). See also Defoe's prescription for tradesmen to give 'every species of goods their trading names' in a 'trading language' which therefore possesses 'the greatest proprieties' (*The Complete English Tradesman* (1725), Letter III, 'Of the Trading Stile', *SW*, p. 227).

12. '*Ecriture* and Eighteenth-Century Fiction', *Literature, Society and*

the Sociology of Literature: Proceedings of the Conference held at the University of Essex, July, 1976, ed. Francis Barker *et al.* (Colchester, 1977), p. 58.

13. For the influence of François, due de la Rochefoucauld's *Maximes* (1665) on the *Verses,* see the poem's sub-title and its opening lines (ll. 1–10, p. 485) and maxims 106 (p. 51), 119 (p. 52), 135 (p. 54) and 458 (p. 95). See also the reprinting of the Locke-Stillingfleet debate of 1698–99, in Probyn (1978b), pp. 166–84.

14. See Paul J. Korshin, 'Probability and Character in the Eighteenth Century', *Probability, Time, and Space in Eighteenth-Century Literature,* ed. Paula R. Backscheider (New York, 1979), pp. 63–77; and Douglas Lane Patey, *Probability and Literary Form: Philosophic Theory and Literary Practice in the Augustan Age* (Cambridge, 1984), pp. 98–125.

4

Drapier

Our present calamities are not to be represented; . . . Numbers of miserable objects crowd our doors, begging us to take their wares at any price, to prevent their families from immediate starving . . . [We] have before our eyes the dismal prospect of universal poverty and desolation. (*The Present Miserable State of Ireland* [1721])

Whether there be upon earth any Christian or civilized people so beggarly, wretched and destitute as the common Irish? (George Berkeley, *The Querist* [1735–37], Query 132)

If we watcht over the breed of our Tenants, or cherisht them as much as those of our Horses, etc. we should soon have Droves of them and labouring Men instead of Bullocks and Sheep. (Dr Samuel Madden, *Reflections and Resolutions* . . . [1738])[1]

These passages are representative of a great body of writing which addressed itself to Irish affairs in the first half of the eighteenth century. Population studies and more accurate econometrics are available to us now, but what matters in this consideration of Swift as the Hibernian Patriot is the intensity of the realisation that a whole community was breaking up. Notice too, though, that Madden's remarks are addressed to the 'Gentlemen' of Ireland, that Berkeley is concerned only about the 'common Irish' and that the anonymous pamphleteer of 1721 is not one of the 'miserable objects' driven to begging. Indeed, his 'dismal prospect' refers more to the *present* scene of desolation than any *future* possibility of this happening to the writer. Unwittingly these writers demonstrate how divided Irish culture was between the beggars and those begged.

Swift himself was quite adamant about this distinction. Indeed neither the Swifts nor his mother's family, the Erricks, were native Irish and it is clear that Swift moved in Anglo-Irish Protestant circles, a class of landlords and political power. The native Irish were conceived as a different breed. Although the one term 'Irish' comprehended both, this was merely a geographical expression. In one of Swift's last surviving letters to Alexander Pope, in June 1737, he reprimands him for treating all Irishmen alike and on not identifying 'the savage old Irish' as distinct from 'the English Gentry of this Kingdom'. Indeed 'the English Colonies' in Ireland are 'much more civilized' than many areas in England, 'and speak better English, and are much better bred' (*Corr.*, 5:58). Swift saw himself either as belonging to both Irish and English cultures, or, increasingly, as at home in neither. Deane Swift, his nephew, and one of his earliest biographers (1755), quotes Swift's assertion that 'he was not born in *Ireland* at all, and ... would insist, that he was stolen from *England* when a child, and brought over to *Ireland* in a band-box' (p. 26). Even his origins he considered hybrid.

This desire to efface his Irishness on the one hand and yet assert it proudly on the other seems like a contradiction. For Swift, however, the Anglo-Irish were acceptable in that they seemed to offer a compromise between English colonialist complacency and Irish barbarism and servility. The 1720s were to see the disintegration of such an ideal in Swift's writing, despite the evidence of his remarks to Pope. In both *The Drapier's Letters* and *A Modest Proposal*, Ireland is a cause of irony and paradox. The historical Ireland of the researcher into parish registers and trade figures cannot deny or support the fertility of Swift's ideological perspective. What it can supply is a glimpse of what, consciously or not, he omits.

Swift's Ireland and English Mercantilism, 1720–30

The evidence for Swift's patriotism depends very heavily on the *Letters* (1724–25) and *A Modest Proposal* (1729). Sheridan in his *Life of Dr. Swift* (1784), reported on the triumphant 'Drapier's' return to England in 1726 as a 'kind of triumph, where he was received and welcomed on shore by a multitude of his grateful countrymen' (p. 261). Four years later, the *Letters* were collected for a London edition as *The Hibernian Patriot*. Instantaneously Swift's 'Drapier' became as much mythical as rhetorical, as much a political rallying-cry as a persona, uniting both the savage and the genteel. Biographical criticism would no doubt argue from the *effects* of Swift's work, its successful campaign against William Wood's royal patent, and conclude that the desperation of *The Modest Proposal* was an eventual failure of hope. Swift's fear of the enemy within Ireland, however, always accompanied his polemics versus the English, and in his Irish tracts of the 1720s, whatever nationalism he explicitly espoused on the one hand was prey to the residual irony on the other that perhaps 'this land of slaves/Where all are fools, and all are knaves' (*Ireland* [1727], ll. 1–2, p. 330) was not worth it. Swift's private misgivings eroded his public professions constantly; the intensity with which this dichotomy was awakened in him on the Irish question however was remarkable.

Swift felt that Irish poverty was manufactured by English mercantilism (the sanctioning of economic war to protect home interests). Ever since Poyning's Law (1494), the Irish Parliament could only convene by English regal assent and so frame its own legislation only when the King and Privy Council pleased. However, the late seventeenth century saw English *economic intervention* legalised. The Navigation Acts of 1663 and 1666 created a monopoly for England in colonial trade and also placed a high tariff on Irish livestock exports to England. In 1699 Irish weavers were forbidden to export finished woollen goods. When, in 1720, the English Parliament passed the Declaratory Act, 'An Act for the better securing the dependency of the Kingdom of Ireland on the crown of Great Britain' by denying Ireland an independent legal system, Ireland's colonial status was assured. There is obviously clear evidence to support Swift's accusations. The Irish Tracts combat English ideologies of imperialism and mercantilism by drawing on a wealth of factual evidence. What adds spice to this, however, is Swift's assertion that, if left to shift for herself, Ireland had the means to be self-sufficient both culturally and economically. As early as 1707, Swift depicted Ireland as an Injured Lady, who although 'born to a good Estate' found that it 'now turneth to little Account' because of the 'Oppressions' she endured (*The Story of the Injured Lady*, IX: 4). In his sermon 'Causes of the Wretched Condition of Ireland' (delivered *c.*1724, published 1762) the opening passage reads like a first draft of the *Proposal*, with the significant exception that the 'very melancholy Reflection' is not just caused by the 'Streets crouded with Beggars' and the sight of 'so many of our lower Sort of Tradesmen, Labourers and Artificers, not able to find Cloaths and Food for their Families', but also the thought that Ireland is capable of self-sufficiency. Indeed, the nation could produce 'sufficient for the support of four Times the Number of its Inhabitants' (IX: 199).[2] The irony of such

SWIFT

contrasts between apparent potential and sordid reality took the form of an irresolvable paradox in much of Swift's Irish writing. One of his most relevant pamphlets was *A Proposal for the Universal Use of Irish Manufacture* (1720), where, as the title suggests, he counsels his fellow Irish to wear only those garments produced at home. The perversity of his fellow countrymen, however, complements English imperialism for 'it is the peculiar Felicity and Prudence of the People in this Kingdom, that whatever Commodities, or Productions, lie under the greatest Discouragements from *England*, those are what they are sure to be most industrious in cultivating and spreading' (IX: 15). The patient, who would otherwise be both hale and hearty, chooses the most expeditious way to die.

Ireland is seen to produce its own rules and expectations, for general maxims of humanity and policy cannot help the analyst make sense of its peculiar problems. In *A Short View of the State of Ireland* (1728), Swift's declared aim not 'to complain, but barely to relate Facts' (XII: 7) promises a transparency of style and thus an objectivity of analysis. Hope of Irish growth however can only introduce paradox, for 'it must be against every Law of Nature and Reason; like the Thorn at *Glassenbury*, that blossoms in the Midst of Winter' (XII: 10). Indeed, 'there is not one Argument used to prove the Riches of *Ireland*, which is not a logical Demonstration of its Poverty' (XII: 11). The savage conclusion to the tract possesses all the intensity of a rhetorical as well as an emotional impasse. The bare factual catalogue of natural advantages is inescapably ironic, 'But my Heart is too heavy to continue this Irony longer' (XII: 10). The plain style in this case becomes almost cosmetic, for its forensic analysis is unnatural, the possession of the comfortable spectator rather than the desperate participator, the almsgiver rather than the beggar at the door. Swift's conclusion to the tract is really an attempt to avoid the paradoxical by affirming where blame lies: with the English, for 'one thing I know, that *when the Hen is starved to Death, there will be no more Golden Eggs*'. Acquisitive English society is responsible for Irish poverty. Paradoxes remove blame because they occur as 'natural' (and so intractable) problems, and as inversions of logic comprehensible purely on an intellectual basis. We cannot 'see' ironies or paradoxes for they arise out of contexts where the visual or physical forms only a part. 'We need not wonder at Strangers, when they deliver such Paradoxes', Swift concludes, 'but a Native and Inhabitant of this Kingdom who gives the same Verdict, must be either ignorant to Stupidity; or a Man-pleaser, at the Expense of all Honour, Conscience and Truth' (XII: 12). Swift feels it his moral duty as an Irishman (honorary or not) to avoid the paradoxical, and yet Irish affairs strike him forcibly as innately ironical, even to the point of paradox. The counsel of the detached spectator is inhumane yet at the same time the means of possible salvation for the 'savage' Irish, whereas the railing of the outraged literate Irishman is natural and yet ultimately unhelpful.

English oppression might also account for Irish distrust of forensic economic remedies. Economic 'projecting', that is, the publication for patent of bright ideas for economic salvation, was a genre that Swift himself had tried. Gulliver was 'a great Admirer of Projects, and a Person of much Curiosity and easy Belief' and indeed had been 'a Sort of Projector' when young (XI: 178). As J. M. Treadwell points out, Swift was a Projector when old too, but very much in the pre-Restoration vein of exhorting *moral* as opposed to *organisational* reform, and also ignoring the clear financial profits that were the contemporary Projector's motive.[3] Daniel Defoe in his *Essay Upon Projects* (1697) attempted to rescue the name for those honest writers who 'turn their thoughts to Honest Invention, founded upon the Platform of Ingenuity and Integrity'. Unfortunately, he testifies at the same time to the more numerous criminal Projector, 'driven by his own desperate Fortune to such a Streight, that he must be delivered by a Miracle, or Starve' (*SW*, pp. 24-5). William Wood and the Modest Proposer are Swift's equivalents for this. The extent to which both biographically or textually Swift distances himself from them is problematic and, indeed, crucial in reading the *Proposal*.

Ireland had often provided projecting subject-matter at a time when the genre of the economic essay was increasingly associated with financial speculation. Most projectors no longer expected royal patronage but rather public subscribers. In its most pejorative sense it could be read as a less direct form of begging. Its rhetoric, however, had found a mode of appearing altruistic and impersonal. In Swift's writings, financial speculation is often closely associated with the insubstantial and the idealistically inhumane. Avarice had been institutionalised. Whilst both Swift and Gay had invested at some time in South Sea stock, the Scriblerians viewed the bursting of the South Sea Bubble in August 1720 as a providential symbol, a sign that the London money market could be as delusive as any Lagadian project. 'Monied' interests associated with the City of London and progressive opportunity, clashed ideologically with 'country' interests, associated with agriculture and Utopian nostalgia.[4] What was principally at stake was a series of priorities: land versus capital and 'humane' reality versus impersonal economism. In his open letter *From Dr. Swift to Mr. Pope* (1721), Swift took as his target 'that scheme of politics ... of setting up a monied interest in opposition to the landed'. The 'possessors of the soil' should be the only judges of what is best for the country. Ownership of the *countryside*, by a semantic sleight-of-hand, comes to signify the proper prerequisite for the distribution of wealth in the *Country*. The enemy is identified as the 'Funds of Credit and South-sea Projects' fostered by Walpole's Whig government (IX: 32). Pope himself was to associate 'Blest paper-credit' with corruption in his *Epistle to Bathurst* (1733), on the grounds that it gave bribes 'lighter wings to fly': 'gold imp'd by thee, can compass hardest things,/Can pocket States, can fetch or carry Kings' (ll. 70–2, p. 574). Proportion and dimension become matters of vulnerable convention, no longer of intrinsic value.

The anonymous pamphleteer of *The Present Miserable State* had made it plain that the South Sea Bubble was a major factor in Irish penury. Swift in his broadside poem *The Bubble* (1721; later known as *Upon the South Sea Project*), transforms the local circumstances into symptoms of social anarchy. Money will be money still, even if viewed through 'a jobber's bill'; 'Put on what spectacles you please,/Your guinea's but a guinea still' (ll. 130–2, p. 211). The South Seas had treacherous deeps and shallows and, for a while, Reason went on holiday, leaving a nation full of mirage-ridden mariners, afloat on watery foundations. Two stanzas were added to the Dublin edition:

> Five hundred chariots just bespoke,
>   Are sunk in these devouring waves,
> The horses drowned, the harness broke,
>   And here the owners find their graves.
>
> Like Pharoah, by directors led,
>   They with their spoils went safe before;
> His chariots tumbling out the dead,
>   Lay shattered on the Red Sea shore.
>   (ll. 33–40, pp. 208–9)

The newly ordered equipage, ordered on South Sea credit, is an unpardonable luxury, analogous to an Egyptian chariot engulfed by the Red Sea—a divine retribution. Such effects of Providence provide a pertinent lesson for the Irish speculators, too apt to pay for their folly by increased rents. It also provides the most sombre detail in the poem, the analogy

103

pairing the social climber of the present with the mendacious
Old Testament pagan ignorant of Divine Order. The world of
credit had, for Swift, usurped the continuity of accepted
definitions based on substance and heredity. Most radical of
all, however, is Swift's view that the very *genus* of humanity
itself plus all the attributes that constitute humanity is
threatened, especially in Ireland. There, along with most
forms of value—'paper-credit', coin and land—people, the
'riches of a nation', are themselves a commodity and thus
undergoing devaluation.[5] In *A Proposal for the Universal Use of
Irish Manufacture*, there is a flawed relation between
commonsense assumptions about human attributes and the
signs of those expectations in *Irish* humans: 'Whoever travels
this Country, and observes the *Face* of Nature, or the *Faces*,
and Habits, and Dwellings of the *Natives*, will hardly think
himself in a Land where either *Law*, *Religion*, or *Common
Humanity* is professed' (IX: 21). 'Professed' is the last twist of
the knife, for it seems that it is only through the 'profession'
of humane activity and order that such qualities can exist in
Ireland. Most certainly they cannot be observed other than in
words, which can perhaps all too easily be merely nominal,
'written' rather than mimetic. Swift's fear of the beast in
mankind took many forms in his writings. In turning to the
composition of *The Drapier's letters* in 1724, it seems that he
was in the process of writing Book III of *Gulliver's Travels*,
having just completed Book IV. The Yahoo and the beggarly
Irish are close relations both at the time of conception in
Swift's work and in their physical resemblance. In *A Letter to
the Archbishop of Dublin, Concerning the Weavers* (1729), body
and soul seem fatally disconnected in Irish life for as he walks
through the streets of Dublin he is driven to reflect

> whether those animals which come in my way with two legs and
> human faces, clad and erect, be of the same species with what I
> have seen very like them in England, as to the outward Shape, but

differing in their notions, natives, and intellectualls more than
any two kinds of Brutes in a forest, which any men of common
prudence would immediately discover, by persuading them to
define what they mean by Law, Liberty, Property, Courage,
Reason, Loyalty or Religion. (XII: 65)

To adopt Locke's distinction, the powers of verbal definition
are limited here because the usual secondary qualities
(rationality and moral behaviour) no longer belong to the
primary human ones ('the outward shape'). When we turn to
Sir William Petty's *Political Arithmetick* (completed 1676;
published 1690), Swift's humanist fear is located against a
backdrop of projecting confidence, the avoidance of
'comparative and superlative Words, and intellectual
Arguments' to attempt only 'Terms of *Number*, *Weight*, or
Measure; to use only Arguments of Sense, and to consider
only such Causes, as have visible Foundations in Nature'
('Preface'). Petty's own *Political Anatomy of Ireland* (completed 1672, published 1691), achieved wide authority in
English political tracts.[6] The 'Anatomy', itself a corporeal/
medical metaphor, could become symptomatic of inhumane
quackery. The only correct response was, for Swift, an ironic
one.

The Drapier's Letters

(a) The Drapier
In choosing a Drapier as his spokesman, Swift chose an
amateur writer. It is also crucial, however, to gauge carefully
the extent to which real Irish drapers' lives could be said to
determine Swift's conscious intentions. Most certainly, Swift
is choosing not to write these letters in the 'writerly' idiom of
the professional essayist. That very choice discloses a desire
to project his polemic against Wood's patent from an
alternative perspective. Swift as 'Drapier' is neither quite

Swift nor a draper. The reader must perceive the fictiveness of the Drapier's series of 'straightforward' confessions of lack of learning or intelligence and yet must appreciate also the passion and enhanced credibility that the Drapier can provide and, for whatever reason, Swift *in propia persona* could not. Just because the Drapier is not directly *mimetic* does not, on the other hand, force a purely *textual* reading on us. Textuality cannot shake itself free of ideology and the material practices to which it alerts us.

The Drapier opposes William Wood and, through him, the Walpole administration, not simply on the pragmatic grounds that the plan to supply £100,800 worth of copper coinage for Ireland (1722) was redundant but because of its symbolic status. The Irish were not consulted and, indeed, before Swift first took up his pen in the cause, both Irish Houses of Parliament had made official protests to the King. Almost immediately it had become a nationalist issue. For Swift, however, the threat was more sinister. In his *Humble Address to both Houses of Parliament* (Letter 7), the lack of halfpence is seen to be a timely occasion for the English to undermine the whole Irish economy further. Base copper coin adulterated for profit by Wood, even if accepted by the coerced Irish, would hardly impress foreign markets, 'Whereby we must infallibly lose all our little Gold and Silver' (X: 125). Furthermore, 'When the Value of Money is *arbitrary*, or *unsettled*; no Man can well be said to have any *Property* at all' (X: 128). The patent is, for Swift, a confluence-point for several issues involving Irish self-determination and English imperialism but perhaps most pervasively, the instability of all values based on financial calculation. In speaking in a Drapier's accents, Swift attempts to overcome the debilitating connotations of both the 'savage' Irish and the criminally negligent absentee landlords, both the illiterate and the irresponsible. In creating an acceptable *via media* in mimetic terms, he also attempts to create a rhetorical authority as well which is grounded on the tangible wealth and craftsmanship of a Drapier's trade, an activity that promises non-written truths and materials but which cannot in effect escape the written at all.

As with Robinson Crusoe's father, the advocacy of middle-class contentment rested on the assumption that it was 'the best State in the World, the most suited to human Happiness, not exposed to the Miseries and Hardships, the Labour and Sufferings of the mechanick Part of Mankind, and not embarrass'd with the Pride, Luxury, Ambition and Envy of the upper Part of Mankind' (p. 4). Crusoe's father, however, could still manage a good estate. The 'middle part' is, however, a useful platform for inaugurating norms of behaviour and taste. 'Upper' or 'lower' can be seen as deviating from the golden mean. Certainly Swift felt that the indigent poor were beyond the pale of rhetoric and charity. The third cause of the 'wretched condition' of Ireland was the 'Idleness and Sloth' of the 'Natives' who 'often chuse to beg or steal, rather than support themselves with their own labour' (IX: 201). When preaching 'On the Poor Man's Contentment', he made a clear distinction between those starving, begging or imprisoned due 'to their own Laziness or Drunkenness,' who do not deserve the name of 'Poor', and 'the honest, industrious Artificer, the meaner Sort of Tradesman, and the Labouring Man' (IX: 191), who are unfortunate indeed. The landlords on the other hand provided the most obvious cause of Irish decline (IX: 200–1). Swift's eulogist in *Verses on the Death of Dr. Swift* (1731) claimed him a friend only of 'a few' and those 'always of the midling kind'. He would pretend not to know the 'Fools of Rank, a mungril; Breed,/Who Fain would pass for Lords indeed' (ll. 439–42, p. 497).

What is stiking, however, about Swift's choice of a draper as spokesman is the Whig pedigree the profession ususally enjoyed. We come now to the thorny problem of whether we can say that Swift was conscious of, and therefore in rational control of, all the consequences of his persona. Lance Bertelsen has recently claimed that 'it was only natural that Swift in combating [Wood's] Coinage, chose for his persona a figure representative of Ireland's continuing victimization by England.'[7] This tallies with the internal evidence but not with a draper's 'worldly' status. The Irish draper acted as the middle-man for the weavers, from whom he received brown linen, and the larger merchants or exporters to whom he sold bleached and finished white cloth. In this, he could have been a figure of a eulogy as Whiggish as Joseph Addison's for the merchant class, who 'knit Mankind together in a mutual Intercourse of good Offices, distribute the Gifts of Nature, find Work for the Poor, add Wealth to the Rich, and magnificence to the Great' (*Spectator* no. 69, 21 May 1711).[8] Conrad Gill dates the emergence of drapers as a distinct class as around 1720, and certainly, thanks to the relaxation of export restrictions on cloth manufacture to England (1696) and the colonies (1705), the Irish linen industry provided a mercantile success story, one of the very few in Ireland at that time.[9] Defoe illustrated Moll Flanders' social pretensions by her marrying a draper, someone who 'was something of a gentleman' as well as a trader, and something of an 'amphibious creature, ... [a] land-water thing called a gentleman-tradesman' (p. 78).

Drapers appeared to be upwardly mobile and this no doubt adds to the uncompromising judgement of William Wood as '*a mean ordinary Man, a Hard-ware Dealer*' (X: 4) and as 'one, single, diminutive insignificant Mechanick' (X: 19) and, especially in the letter to the '*Nobility and Gentry of the Kingdom of Ireland*' (Letter 3), as a social parvenu with aspirations to have 'Esq.' after his name in the patent 'although he were understood to be only a Hard-ware-Man' (X: 129). Such confidence expresses itself in the solid materialism of a comfortable employment. 'I am no inconsiderable Shop-Keeper in this Town' (X: 16), he declares, and then often refers the reader to the visible stock upon which his wealth is based: 'I have a pretty good Shop of *Irish Stuffs* and *Silks*' (X: 7), or 'I can live better than many others: I have some Gold and Silver by me, and a Shop well furnished' (X: 22). This materialism is both a cause of pride at one turn and of self-effacement at another, for when addressing his betters, the Drapier dubs himself 'an *illiterate Shop-Keeper*' who has had no 'help of books' but rather has 'endeavoured ... to improve that small Portion of Reason, which God hath pleased to give [him]; and when Reason plainly appears before [him]; [he] cannot turn away [his] Head from it' (X: 28). It seems that the Drapier, because he is no bookman, is therefore to be trusted. His writing will involve as much fair trading as the sale of '*Irish Stuffs* and *Silks*'.

These rhetorical traits of 'character' are extrapolated from the mimetic consequences of the persona. 'M. B. Drapier' is not reducible, on the other hand, to a draper *tout court*. 'M. B.' has recently been interpreted as an acronym for Marcus Brutus, the central figure in the plot to murder Julius Caesar and thus a symbol of courageous resistance to tyranny.[10] The Drapier as David confronted by the Goliath of an established and powerful Whig government is consistent with this (X: 48). There is also a wider satirical function suggested by the name. Sir William Temple implied a now obsolete meaning for 'to drape' as 'to satirise' from the French *draper*, but there are other possible meanings: (a) the action of weaving cloth, (b) to cover with or adorn artistically as well as the more directly mimetic (c) to trade in cloth. A draper deals in fashionable adornment yet also has the chance to strip off the superficial and get at the essential human beneath. Turn this prismatic symbol a little and the reader sees a skilful weaver of words who, in the very process of constructing his address to shopkeeper and noble, is a *rhetor* in the classical tradition. Here is no simple claim to truth set against artifice; Swift's 'Drapier' adorns only to expose and constructs only to destroy. In the *Letters*, the no-nonsense tradesman has an advantage over even a literate Anglo-Irish clergyman. Unencumbered with bookish figures of speech, he finds it easier to escape the paradoxes to which a specifically *ethical* stance led Swift *in propria persona*.

As we have seen in the case of his Irish tracts, Swift was well aware of the ironies of Irish history, and in making his stand as the Drapier, he attempts to elude them by a gesture of affirmation at a time when he felt the reduced accuracy of an abstract vocabulary—at least, in reference to the Irish. That he could not escape from the overarching irony of the practice he had to choose and the history he could not choose but experience, was no defeat. He did, after all, prevent the enactment of Wood's patent.

(b) The 'Terms of Art'

Many recent literary critics have either seized on the *Letters* as historical documentation alone or as superb political rhetoric. In both cases, the procedural ironies of Swift's undertaking have seemed largely beside the point. The reassurance of determinate historical ends (the defeat of William Wood's patent) has formed a desire to find in them consistency and organic unity. W. B. Ewald, Jr praises the Drapier for 'being equal to any emergency. Despite a few exceptions, it is with astonishing consistency that Swift continually fits his arguments to his *persona*. Even in the instances where it appears that Swift himself is speaking, ... the humble Drapier always appears to reinforce Swift's message' (p. 119). Oliver W. Ferguson feels that 'the Drapier was only a shadow, but he was a shadow cast by the familiar and reassuringly concrete figure of the Dean of St Patrick's (p. 98). F. P. Lock has most recently observed that

Swift 'went to unusual pains to create the Drapier as a credible fictive author', even if the mask is 'always patently a mask' (1983, pp. 164–5). Even J. A. Downie, who finds that the adoption of the persona has attracted undue attention, is aware of the division between the 'Dean' and the 'Drapier' in the work, for, aside from the use of 'homely Biblical allusion' addressed to tradesmen, 'there is no real attempt to give substance to the Drapier's character' and, indeed, such a device is not as realised as Gulliver, for example, because no attempt is made 'to parody the style of his own persona'. Indeed, Swift 'was doing little more than thinly veiling his own authorship of the piece' (pp. 238–9). In these summaries, the critic/reader is aware, sometimes disturbingly so, of a duet between Dean, the consummate rhetorician, and Drapier, a part of his rhetoric. The one underpins the other and both present a united front. Intention emerges unscathed from its dangerously written form.

One does not have to espouse deconstruction to offer a less reassuring account of the *Letters'* textuality. Claude Rawson has been most timely in pointing to the predominantly rhetorical nature of both 'Dean' and 'Drapier'. The alternation between the two is hardly disturbing for the reader of satire, though it must be doubly so for those expecting novelistic conventions. The 'worry' is caused 'not so much by inconsistencies of character, as by tones of voice'. It is the 'unctuous overplaying' of the falsely naive or, to take the argument further, the urgency of the preaching or the occasional (and surprising) descent into indecorously physical metaphors that is truly disturbing' (1973, p. 30). The separation of 'Dean' from 'Drapier' is only one split out of several and to treat the *Letters* as either history or rhetoric is to ignore such meanders the better to plot a more straightforward course. As Rawson points out, with particular relevance to Swift, authors readily fall into certain 'tones of voice' that express 'a prevailing atmosphere rather than their own personal, professional or political predispositions, or at least' they enter 'into curious combinations with these predispositions' (p. 36). This unenunciated 'atmosphere' is not just a cloak to preserve Swift from legal redress, but also an ironical textuality, where no one guise or paraphrasable meaning is comfortable and where the crisis in all evaluation is explored through this one historical instance of Wood's attempted devaluation of the currency. Thus, whilst the 'Drapier' may claim to confront the reader with material 'fact', he is quite ostentatiously weaving a fabric out of such materials, and 'dressing' his own chosen point of view in certain rhetorical 'fabrics' to win general assent. The claim that he is merely expounding a truth obvious to his audience's common sense achieves its clarity by way of skill and rhetorical cunning. The art by which artifice is hidden is still art.

The Drapier's forceful 'presence' is often an effect of his claim to speak plainly. In his *Letter to the Shop-Keepers* (Letter 1), the Drapier's fellow traders are to be confronted by the '*plain Story of the Fact*' of Wood's patent (X: 4), an *aide-mémoire* that 'all Families' should keep by them (X: 12). The gentry in Letter 3, are to be convinced by a shopkeeper who, although '*illiterate*', can identify the reasonable when it 'plainly appears before [him]'. All that's left the Drapier is 'plain Reason, unassisted by Art, Cunning, or Eloquence' (X: 28-9). The whole crisis should be presented 'nakedly, as it lies before us' (X: 57), and, indeed, if such a description were published 'that none could mistake it', it 'would be of a infinite Ease and Use to the Kingdom, and either prevent or silence all Discontents' (X: 108). Just as reason immediately strikes the Drapier as truth, the reader should be similarly convinced by a plainness that brooks no controversy.

Free interpretation, the privatising of otherwise consensual meanings, is as much a foe for Swift as Wood's unbalancing of Irish monetary values. A shopkeeper takes coin of the realm on trust that it serves as an equivalent token for others. 'Paper-credit' had recently been discredited. Wood's patent threatened to undermine the trust in all currency until the exchange system of bartering was the only alternative. Verbal exchange functions for Swift on the same contractual trust. Wherever possible the Drapier, used to weaving raw materials, transforms his writing into similar material. Besides an aid to memory, his pamphleteering becomes, for example, a cordial 'that must be frequently applied to weak Constitutions, *Political* as well as *Natural*' (X: 53), 'a Piece of *black and white Stuff*, just sent from the *Dyer*' (*A Proposal for the Universal Use of Irish Manufacture*) or, is '*plain, strong, coarse stuff*' for 'the *lower and poorer Sort of People*' (Letter 1) which 'preserved many Thousands from Agues' (X: 82–3). Swift is at pains to deny in his own writing the elusiveness of a single meaning and the rhetorical conditions of all written reasoning.

Writing is an unfortunate realm of artifice. Answering Whig legislation point by point, the Drapier frequently exposes its nominal authority. In, *A Letter to the Whole People of Ireland* (Letter 4), the precedent of calling Ireland a '*depending Kingdom*', that is, subservient to England, is redefined as 'a *modern Term of Art*; unknown, as I have heard, to all antient *Civilians*, and *Writers upon Government*' (X: 62). The clinching proof is the aside 'I have heard', an utterance and not a written phrase, a maxim from an impersonal gnomic wisdom not the private plan of an individual writer. Swift, by becoming something he is not in assuming the mantle of the Drapier, is actually transcending the particular and the biased. Even when wielding a pen for the defence of liberty, that most ideal and ecumenical of causes, the Drapier or his surrogate, steps back from its implications of fictiveness and individual creation. The new writer of Letter 6 even doubts whether one can identify the Drapier as responsible for the previous controversial letter, finding 'little to the Purpose' such purely *legal* questions of identity. He likewise will have to watch carefully 'every Stroke of [his] Pen, and venturing only to incur the publick Censure of the World as a Writer; not of [his] Lord Chief Justice *Whitshed*, as a Criminal'. What is more the quibbles of ingenuity, the 'Terms of Art' that include *'Poining's* Act; ... Subordination; Dependence' belong purely to the *written* order 'which I shall not contest, but am too dull to understand' (X: 111–12). This 'dullness' is at one with his non-writerly trade and is hardly culpable. Faced with the personal associations that attach themselves to any statement, the Drapier instils confidence in the reader to trust to the commonsensical, even clichéed meanings that immediately suggest themselves. Writing for the Drapier is a function, not self-expression. The preacherly (and vocative) moods of Letter 1 seat the reader in a congregation, not his/her own study. The second-person addressed in the letter is always plural. Indeed, the whole genre of the 'letter', no matter how open or public its actual publication was, is an opportunity for spoken accents and the immediacy of personal contact. Therefore, the 'trade' of writing is distinguished from more reputable commerce such as the retailing of cloth and wool. The Drapier increasingly laments the 'Trade of a Writer' (X: 81), and wonders, therefore, at the great 'Provocation' that 'could stir up an obscure, indolent *Drapier*, to become an *Author*' (X: 88). By the end of *A Letter to ... the Lord Viscount Molesworth* (Letter 5), his 'Office as a Writer' has grown burdensome, not because the cause he has supported had disappointed him but rather because he inadvisedly 'chose to *appeal* to *Law* and *Liberty*, and *the common Rights of Mankind*, without considering the *Climate* [he] was in' (X: 93). Writing is therefore not only a snare for the innocent reader, but also for the innocent writer. The public sphere, once the possessor of clear definitions of morals and laws, can turn mendacious for its own ends. As the Drapier confesses in *A Letter to the Lord Chancellor Midleton* (Letter 6), perhaps he might have been better employed 'in looking to his Shop' or in writing 'Proverbs' or 'Ballads' instead of pamphlets (X: 110).

The Drapier is not only free of culpable motives; his very words must also exhibit such purity of intention and signification. He is frequently clarifying and grounding his meaning by appealing to a consensus. It is precisely because of their lack of a spontaneous morality and knowledge of their own interest, that the Irish people need such written cordials. When interpreting the words 'Voluntary' and 'Willing to receive it' used to describe the liberty of the Irish to receive the new coinage, the Drapier directs the reader to the 'true natural Meaning, *as commonly understood by PROTESTANTS*' (X: 45). When defending himself to Viscount Molesworth against his accusers, he expresses indiscreet Protestant zeal, a defence he doubts not but that 'some People would wrest . . . to an ill Meaning, by a spiteful Interpretation' (X: 86). On quoting impeccable Whig sentiments concerning the protection of Liberty and Property as his defence against the Whig government, he believes them 'Words of Known Use and Signification in this Kingdom' despite the empty mouthings of lawyers (X: 87), the same lawyers who might 'distort or extend' his meaning when referring to 'the People' (X: 103). This is not only the plain style of the common man, but an insistent desire to escape the rhetorical deceptions of writing.

Repeatedly the necessary idealism which should bind the Irish people to concerted action collides in the *Letters* with a world of power which owns words and their power to define reality. As with the political projectors in Lagado, mere words, even if plainly expressed, can be invaded by alien meanings. This is clearest in Letter 6, one of the 'prepared' letters for his *Works*. In writing to the Lord Chancellor Midleton, Swift disowns his guise as the Drapier. The

'*Advertisement* to the *Reader*' claims that Swift's name appeared at the bottom of the unpublished pamphlet 'although blotted out by some other Hand' (X: 97). This teasing disavowal of responsibility disperses authorship. This particular letter is only to see the light of day because of an editor's intervention; a ploy Swift had used in the early days of the Drapier. The writer of Letter 6 can safely treat the Wood's patent events as history as he is entering 'at the latter End of a Debate' (X: 99), and so escaping the notoriety of the Drapier who had been caught up in the local events of that time. Words have some weight it would seem for writers can be legally accountable for them. Religious or moral subjects can be topics of controversy in print, but not from the pulpit. The new 'Drapier' does not consider the issues here 'an Affair of State, until Authority shall think fit to declare it so' (X: 100). Swift is here zig-zagging away from his words, lending them an impersonal force. Mimetically, his elusiveness is self-protection, for no amount of ethical or religious fervour will prevent his writing entering the realm of civil affairs. Rhetorically, on the other hand, it is a form of self-display, by emphasising the writer's Olympian ethos. Determined to 'relate the naked Fact, as it stands in the View of the World' (X: 105), he must also divorce himself from the very 'World', the public, so as to be a 'Stranger to Affairs' (X: 106). The price of a reliable literary personality is the reduction of a Juvenalian *saeva indignatio*.

The politics of this 'rhetorical' position cannot be annexed to a safe Toryism. For once true to a predictable mercantilist position, the Drapier refuses an author's authority (greater *savoir faire* or learning than the reader) in most of the letters after Letter 1. His book learning is *seen* to be acquired and his political acumen is a response to the government's display of power. If anything, his responses are liberal, not the authoritarian ones we habitually expect. In *A Letter to Mr. Harding* (Letter 2), the Drapier is confident that the law will be the people's safeguard against an unjust Royal Proclamation (X: 21). When addressing the gentry in Letter 3, he is bolder in this claim, limiting 'the King's *Prerogative*' by 'the *Good* and *Welfare* of his *People*' (X: 34); law and the state's apparatuses to enforce it become an expression of temporal power. This is clear in Letter 3 where, quoting St Paul (I Cor. 6:xii), an action's lawfulness (a temporal enactment) need not coincide with its 'expediency' or necessity (X: 41). Indeed, precedents, the lawyer's stock-in-trade, need not be binding because the particular set of circumstances that provoked them leave them as of only relative status. The 'Necessity, or Turbulence, or Iniquity of Times' can appropriate perfectly innocent meanings or use innocence to cloak the most malicious partiality (X: 40). Lagadian machinations leave the status of the written word malleable and flexible. Lawyers such as Sir William Scroggs could discover 'much more than ever the Authors intended' (X: 92). This partial and tendentious act of interpretation must not be mirrored by similarly subjective language on the Drapier's part. By appealing to the Whig watchwords of Liberty and Property, especially against the Whig Lord Viscount Molesworth in Letter 5, the Drapier wishes on his reader a consensual reading and an effort to appreciate the blessings of '*Liberty . . . to which the whole Race of Mankind hath an Original Title; whereof nothing but unlawful Force can divest them*' (X: 86). Wood indeed can claim the force of royal preferment. He cannot, however, take a stand on reasonable principles.

Swift's Irish tracts had stressed and were to stress the instability of all Irish definitions both natural classifications and written ones. As the Irish people were to suffer the diminution of material degradation, the hopes for moral transcendence were necessary if unreasonable given the English laws that conditioned the 'savage Irish'. The delusive words of English jurisdiction were at war with the fictitious

Drapier, but Swift's persona is not a fiction in the same way that Poyning's Act or the Navigation Acts were. The Drapier is rhetorical, a means to indicate history whilst not joining its compromises and divisions. Such an 'innocent' character, however, could still highlight them by asking awkward questions: 'Am I a *Free-man* in *England,* and do I become a *Slave* in six hours, by crossing the Channel?' (X: 31). Words could make it so.

The Modest Proposal and the Rhetorical Manner

The economic projector responsible for proposing a final solution to Irish poverty is also something of a rhetorician. So apparently controlled does the *Proposal* read that the New Critical phase of Swift criticism delighted in the ironic artistry Swift exercised. W. B. Ewald, Jr, for example, finds Swift (not the Projector) delivering idealistic hopes, invigorated by their negative expression. These are 'incorporated in the measures which the author rejects as impossible ... a positive satiric and ethical message, heightened and intensified, not obscured by the irony, is present in the *Modest Proposal*' (pp. 173–4). The irony is therefore *functional* in that it is a design by which altrusim may be alerted both to the temporising blandness it could easily become and to the real need for effective charity. The ironical passages, once inverted semantically, become a bitter reproach to English mercantilism and a clarion call to Irish brotherhood (the polar opposite to Irish cannibalism). Martin Price, although less stirred by its polemical clarity, still finds in Swift a master craftsman, implicating the unwary reader in misreading the 'surface irony' and therefore involving him/her in a 'comedy of iresponsible folly' where the 'guilt of most men' is eventually discovered as the Proposer taints 'more and more of us in his own madness' (1953, p. 74). The most exteme pronouncement on the *Proposal*'s coherence, however, can be found in Charles A. Beaumont's rhetorical reading, where he traces a fairly accurate generic pattern: that of the classical oration, where 'a revolutionary new proposal is insinuated in a traditional, respected form' (p. 16). The classical requirement of the 'ethical proof' (where only if we are convinced we are listening to a morally good orator are we liable to agree with his proposals) is travestied as we realise how much the diminution of humankind is being supported by Projecting 'ethics'.

Beaumont's analysis, therefore, identifies the immoral proposer as distinct from Swift. The classical oration, once founded on the substantial *ethos* of character and 'his/her' personal verbal contact with the listener, crumbles once an immoral orator adopts its ground rules as a matter of good form alone. Econometric discourse was all too apt to divorce the humane from the statistical, the classical *ethos* from the oratory that once gave it shape and power. However, where both Ewald and Price found the *Proposal* a shared responsibility, Beaumont discovers the solo 'voice' of the Proposer: 'Swift has fully exploited the possibilities of this proof [the ethical] by his thorough development of the character of the projector, whose personality is evident either implicitly or explicitly in every paragraph of the essay' (p. 42). Irony, however, is a mode of writing that deliberately disturbs 'inner' and 'outer'. There is always a residual uncertainty that even if we faithfully understand the opposite of what is expressed we are indeed receiving a positive moral ideal and are therefore travelling towards the heart of the text. In the *Proposal* those elements which seem to compose only the superficies of the writing, the extraneous objectivity of the style, say, or the inhumane rationality, cannot be erased easily just by comprehending only what must have been meant by the writer. The emotional complexion of the text rests with its ironic statements. No satisfying, full-blooded 'presence'

119

(as supplied by the New Critics) can quite heal this division between the outrage at the surface suggestions and the intention deduced from them. The delay between the emotional and the intellectual is crucial. Some would want to deny this shock its anarchy. C. N. Manlove, for instance, admires Swift's satiric potency which drives the reader to 'reconcile ... opposites in our lives even where it exposes their disjunction; and, in the fusion of reason and energy in its procedure, enacts, on a literary level at least, something of the harmony it challenges us to find' (p. 124). F. R. Leavis was far less sanguine about the *Proposal*'s 'remarkably disturbing energy' which induces 'a trust in the solid ground before opening the pitfall' (p. 77). This rhetorical trap uses mimetic considerations for a textual purpose. Ultimately the *Proposal* would seem to signify through its effect on the reader not by a homiletic coherence that immediately indicates the world and its inherited structures.

The Character of the Projector

When the projector outlines the economic effect of his *Proposal* he is at pains to stress how English trade in meat will be unaffected: 'For, this kind of Commodity will not bear Exportation; the Flesh being of too tender a Consistence, to admit a long Continuance in Salt'. This over-solicitude forms part of the Projector's sycophantic desire to sell his product. However, the very next clause cannot easily support such a consistent reading:' *although, perhaps, I could name a Country, which would be glad to eat up our whole Nation without it*' (XII: 117). The italics are a warning signal, for the sudden metaphorical analogy between the 'savage' Irish eating their own children and the English, through economic domination devouring Ireland, is surely not calculated to curry favour with potential English patrons. All irony cast aside, it would

appear that Swift speaks directly here. The disturbing aspect
of the *Proposal* is its sudden, unannounced changes of
speaker, or, to speak 'textually', its conflicting styles of
discourse. Swift becomes the Projector just for the final
clause, but it is enough to engender a fruitful uncertainty as to
who is speaking and, more generally, as to how much we can
rely on reading the *whole* text as ironic.

This is a doubt which is a result of two realignments that
the reader has to assess. First, there is the shock in paragraph
9 that the Projector's economic logic will not scruple to
prescribe cannibalism. So carefully and reasonably has he
detailed his argument and so aggrieved has he been at the
'*helpless Infants*' of paragraph 1 (XII: 109), the '*poor innocent
Babes*' and the '*present Distresses of the Kingdom*' of paragraphs
5 and 6, that we are led to believe that the 'Tears and Pity'
which might move 'the most Savage and inhuman Beast' (XII:
110) are much more than a matter of form. The Projector's
own phrases remain on the record to be used against him. It is
he who speaks of savagery, inhumanity, the innocence of the
eaten, and national distress. By an ironic inversion the reader
can propose a rather orderly hypothesis: that Swift is engaging
his sympathies against both English econometrics and its
quantifying of human life as statistical evidence. There are
further ironies that arise out of this radical reversal of
sympathies. The Projector's expectations of material advantage and national fame illustrate the divisiveness of Irish
social life, the chasm between those Irish who propose
economic remedies in English terms and the 'savage Irish'
who must suffer them. There is also the possibility that the
Projector's dispassionate descriptions of humanity instil
doubt as to his validity before paragraph 9. The repugnantly
physical 'Child *just dropt from its Dam*' clashes awkwardly with
the spiritual 'Souls in *Ireland*'. Mothers become 'Breeders' and
indulge in the 'lawful Occupation of *Begging*' whereas their
offspring earn their livelihood by theft, an '*Art*' with its own

'*Probationers*' (XII: 110–11). Such *laissez-faire* description is really a passive acceptance of human degradation. Begging and theft once safely installed within the social structure perpetuate themselves and also appear a natural, even if regrettable, phenomenon.

These are comforting conclusions, but also a little premature. The irony is a little more complex at the close of the text. At paragraph 29, the Projector claims that such remedies are proposed only for Ireland '*and for no other that ever was, is, or I think ever can be upon Earth*'. There follows a comprehensive list of exactly those measures that Swift from 1720 onwards had advised the Irish people to adopt such as '*utterly rejecting the Material and Instruments that promote foreign Luxury*' or '*teaching Landlords to have, at least, one Degree of Mercy towards their Tenants*' (XII: 116). The Projector may put them by dismissively, but these 'Expedients' seem deduced from common expectations of human activity—not Irish ones. What is more the catalogue is disproportionately lengthy for one who had earlier seemed to brook no objection or alternative to his scheme. The Projector's negatives seem to be losing their potency and their plausibility. A double negative is not quite the same as a positive statement, as it clearly admits an alternative and displays the act of will demanded in rejecting it.

The last four paragraphs, indeed, describe the desperate circumstances peculiar to Ireland and also introduce a Projector 'wearied out for many years with offering vain, idle, visionary Thoughts' and who 'fell upon' this solution because it was '*solid* and *real*, of no Expense, and little Trouble, full in our own Power'. Only when he enjoys a 'Glimpse of Hope' can he once again believe that 'some hearty and sincere Attempt' to adopt rational solutions will prevail and the Irish will 'put them in Practice' (XII: 117). This characterisation may just about agree with the opening assurances of evenhandedness and public service but by this point in the text the ironic mediation is at its thinnest, if only because the genre of the Proposal form and our confidence in the illusionistic validity of the persona have both been questioned. The last paragraph, far from demonstrating the Projector's disinterested sincerity (which is what he professes), seems like a return to the confidence of the opening passages. Read 'textually', and not 'mimetically', the closing apology is actually self-defeating. No child of his will be eaten as his wife is too old to bear children and his youngest is too old to be volunteered for the experiment. The test of his disinterestedness is the lack of material advantage in this, but, at the same time, the proof of his self-interest lies in his prescribing for others what he does not risk himself. We cannot entertain both conclusions here in some balanced synthesis. The Projector cannot be both altruistic and (now) desperate on the one hand and calculatedly scheming on the other.

The Mixed Mode of A Modest Proposal

These contradictory aspects of human characterisation suggest eventually what the Projector's rhetoric might have led us to expect in the first place: that the 'Projector' is no more than a textual effect which exploits our instructive desire to identify with the first-person in most kinds of writing. This convention contributes to the closing *aporia*, where the satire points at more generally held attitudes and their rhetorical gloss and apology. The euphonious 'reason' of the Projector's measured cadences is rendered suspicious because it is associated with measuring of another sort, an inhumane economic quantification of life itself.

Consider, therefore, the clash of styles in the following passages:

There is likewise another great Advantage in my *Scheme*, that it will prevent those *voluntary Abortions*, and that horrid Practice of *Women murdering their Bastard Children*; alas! too frequent among us; sacrificing the *poor innocent Babes*, I doubt, more to avoid the Expence than the Shame; which would move Tears and Pity in the most Savage and inhuman Breast. (XII: 110)

I am assured by our Merchants, that a Boy or a Girl before twelve Years old, is no saleable Commodity; and even when they come to this Age, they will not yield above Three Pounds, or Three Pounds and half a Crown at most, on the Exchange; ...

I shall now therefore humbly propose my own Thoughts; which I hope will not be liable to the least Objection.

I have been assured by a very knowing *American* of my Acquaintance in *London*; that a young healthy Child, well nursed, is, at a Year old, a most delicious, nourishing, and wholesome Food; whether *Stewed, Roasted, Baked*, or *Boiled*; and, I make no doubt that it will equally serve in a *Fricasie*, or *Ragoust*. (XII: 111)

Outrageous suggestions war with a syntactical and discursive orderliness. The definition of mothers murdering their illegitimate offspring as a 'horrid Practice', is at best redundant, at worst an unwitting indication that such verbalising disguises or aims to attenuate the horror of the action itself. 'Tears and Pity' do not flow but rather statements that they should. Similarly, the nice distinctions and quoting of authorities that connote impersonality in the second passage introduce a concomitant lack of humane responsibility which is fully realised perhaps only at the word 'Food'. The clauses that surround this trigger-word proliferate either in delaying adjectival constructions or redundant elaboration on culinary themes. The degree of the Projector's certitude ('I have been assured ...', 'I make no doubt') promotes, ironically, the reader's uncertainty about his morality and the style it adopts.

Both the *Proposal* and the *Letters* can suddenly break the decorum of an abstract verbal norm. What Leavis perceived as 'an effect directly upon ourselves' in the *Proposal* is the structural irony of bureaucratic pedantry usurped by 'the feelings appropriate to rejection' (p. 77). This is a flexible dichotomy. Sometimes the pedant can be the connoisseur of appearances as well: 'Those who are more thrifty (*as I must confess the Times require*) may flay the Carcase; the Skin of which, artificially dressed, will make admirable *Gloves for Ladies* and *Summer Boots for fine Gentlemen*.' The 'virtue' of thrift can ordain the flaying of carcases to supply luxuries which create 'Persons of Quality' (XII: 112). In a demonic complementarity the very essential qualities that define a human being (the smooth skin that provides facial characteristics and 'dresses' the flesh-and-bones) are redistributed to provide the essentials of fashionable quality, a *jeunesse doré* but in an unexpected sense.

In the *Letters*, such abstraction and particularity work alternately. Frequently, the particular instance becomes energetic denunciation and an example of the oppressive reality that no theory can chart. When illustrating how the English government had sometimes bound the Irish by their own laws, the Drapier cites the unavailing opposition of William Molyneux and others whose writings had exposed 'Truth, Reason, and Justice' (X: 62). Facts, however, will always betray the abstract principles that should provide their true context:

> For in *Reason*, all *Government* without the Consent of the *Governed*, is the *very Definition of Slavery*: but in *Fact*, *Eleven Men well armed, will certainly subdue one single Man in his Shirt*. But I have done. For those who have used *Power* to cramp *Liberty*, have gone so far as to resent even the *Liberty* of *Complaining*; although a Man upon the Rack, was never known to be refused the Liberty of *roaring* as loud as he thought fit. (X: 63)

Paradoxically, Swift's prose is unfettered by particular instances of coercion and restrained when discoursing reasonably about the possibilities of liberty. In the *Proposal* the separate styles are more obviously antagonistic. The 'Infants Flesh' that furnishes '*merry Meetings*' (XII: 116), the 'prime Dainty' for '*Persons of Quality*' that is really a Formosan child's carcase (XII: 113) or the 'Child' that will 'make two Dishes' (XII: 112) are grotesque juxtapositions. As in the *Tale*, the typographical resource of italics reinforces this sense of dislocation. The coherence of the Projector's personal accents is disturbed by an accentuation which does not follow speech patterns but rather the dictates of a third party that committed them to print. Therein lies the outrage at what would be a particularly Irish distribution of wealth and also the blindness of its eminently sane practitioners. An unbridled reaction would provide a loose catalogue of graphic details that both enact and describe the disintegration of cultural order. The sudden intensities of italics betray the Projector's madness by exposing his unacknowledged inhumanity and the empty stylistic flourishes that express its merely nominal morality.

Swift's Irish Tracts are not uniformly partisan. As Claude Rawson has recently emphasised, a sternly Protestant aversion to Papist populousness works against his otherwise Irish defence of the poor against both the Anglo-Irish and the English (Hilson, pp. 29–33, 44–5).[11] Whilst the beggars are undeserving, they still deserve far more than they receive from absentee landlords and English mercantilism. The power of an abstract vocabulary is significantly weak, not only mimetically (in that Irish affairs are anarchic anyway) but also rhetorically, for the Tracts' energy is a result of the visceral usurping the spiritual, or the particular 'fact' disproving powerless 'reason'. This need not be contrived into an 'organic unity' or rescued by recourse to a stable ego of an 'author'. Mimetically, they can certainly be read as polemical prose against English interference in Irish affairs, but the 'coherence model' does less than justice to their mercurial surprises and disturbing irrationalities. Irvin Ehrenpreis' reading of the *Proposal* (and personae in general) emphasises the rational control of a discoverable 'Jonathan Swift'. His literary disguises are 'deliberately intended to be penetrated' and so emerge as a 'method of stating, not hiding, what one thinks' (1974, p. 59). From one perspective, this is correct in that the whole work is constituted an entity by its publishing history and attributed to Swift by its appearance in the third volume of *Miscellanies* (1732) and the fourth volume of his *Works* (1735). This seems a very minimal discovery, for the function of some authoritative norm such as an 'author' might aid the cataloguer, but cannot account for the occasions in one's reading where 'meaning', 'author' and 'reader' are most unstable referents. Ehrenpreis believes that 'only as a relationship between a real speaker and a real listener can meaning exist' (p. 60). Such meaning is conceived only as stable and ultimately consistent, something deduced as the text's aim after its wild divagations have finally been discounted. This is reassuring for those who find themselves anxious at the 'new and alarming procedures with new and alarming results' in the analysis of 'the nature of human identity' (p. 49). Swift found himself similarly confronted by such disturbing novelty, but could not ignore it with such complacency. The result is a series of texts which betray both radical uncertainty and a desire to overcome it. It is this coruscating textuality rather than any stated meaning that ensures their renewed relevance.

Notes

1. *The Prose Works of Jonathan Swift, D. D.*, ed. Temple Scott (London, 1908), 7:164; *The Works of George Berkeley, Bishop of Cloyne*, ed. A. A. Luce and T. E. Jessop (London, 1953), 6:116; *Reflections and Resolutions Proper for the Gentlemen of Ireland, as*

to their Conduct for the Service of their Country (Dublin, 1738), p. 51.

2. For a less optimistic opinion of Ireland's self-sufficiency, see L. M. Cullen, *Anglo-Irish Trade 1660–1800* (Manchester, 1968), pp. 46–7, 58–9, and *An Economic History of Ireland since 1660* (London, 1972),pp. 34–40.

3. 'Jonathan Swift: The Satirist as Projector', *Texas Studies in Literature and Language*, 17 (1975), 439–60.

4. For a fuller account, see H.T. Dickinson, *Liberty and Property: Political Ideology in Eighteenth-Century Britain* (London, 1977), pp.169–75, and W. A. Speck, *Society and Literature in England 1700–60* (Dublin, 1983), pp. 116–38.

5. The fate of this cliché and its widespread currency is described in Louis Landa, '*A Modest Proposal* and Populousness', *Modern Philology*, 40 (1942), 161–70.

6. *The Economic Writings of Sir William Petty*, ed. Charles H. Hull (Cambridge, 1899), 1:244. The *Anatomy* can be found at 1: 121–31.

7. 'Ireland, Temple, and the Origins of the Drapier', *Papers on Language and Literature*, 13 (1977), 413–19.

8. *The Spectator*, ed. Donald F. Bond (Oxford, 1965), 1:296.

9. *The Rise of the Irish Linen Industry* (Oxford, 1925), pp. 51–60.

10. See Jack Gilbert, 'The Drapier's Initials', *Notes and Queries*, 208 (1963), 217–18.

11. This was first pointed out by David Nokes (1976). See also his 'The Radical Conservatism of Swift's Irish Pamphlets', *British Journal of Eighteenth-Century Studies*, 7 (1984), 169–76; and Rawson (1980).

Conclusion

Throughout this study a distinction has been observed between 'mimetic' and 'textual' readings, the one stressing how Swift's writing reflected an external world of public affairs and political affiliation, the other denying (evenually) the truth of any such reflection. Consequently, the 'textual' critic emphasises the metaphorical life of the work, a vitality too contradictory and carnivalistic to be judged by what could be considered extrinsic criteria, such as 'intention', 'ideology' or historical/literary 'context'. The one is primarily an aid to judgement and explanation, the other to enjoyment.

These alternatives continually restate some of the working principles of either the biographical or 'New Critics mentioned in Chapter 1, with one crucial difference; the Post-Structuralist is far more sceptical about the truth of the extrinsic approach than the New Critics ever were, and would even deny a coherence to the written work. In contrast, Cleanth Brooks, for example, when dwelling on lyric poetry as his major fund of literary *exempla*, returns constantly to the unity of literary creation:

to deny that the coherence of a poem is reflected in a logical paraphrase of its 'real meaning' is not, of course, to deny coherence to poetry; it is rather to assert that its coherence is to be sought elsewhere. The characteristic unity of a poem (even of those poems that may accidentally possess a logical unity as well as a poetic unity) lies in unification of attitudes into a hierarchy, subordinated to a total and governing attitude.[1]

Textuality not only runs counter to logical design but also to the 'governing attitude' that may unify the text at the expense of its unparaphrasable details—an attitude not only deduced from the text but also consistently imposed on it by the critic. This more thoroughgoing textual approach it has not been my aim to practise here for two reasons: first, I feel that contextualising Swift, or rather the work which bears that signature, is more exciting than ignoring historical testimony (and our efforts to make sense of it) by turning all into linguistic effects, and secondly, in relation to Swift in particular, the ambiguities that thwart any clear critical exposition of his views in *Gulliver* and the *Tale* are often fully appreciated in all of their paradoxical vigour only when set against contemporary preoccupations and events. In short, this study is 'mimetic' in its attempts to supply causal explanations for Swift's writing.

However, there are still virtues in incorporating 'textual' readings into literary history. Far too frequently, the significant texts for historians *tout court*, or historians of ideas, are those which form coherent patterns such as in lines of influence or the development of a particular style. Taking a mass of texts, perhaps over a long period, such critics choose to emphasise their similarities or to tease out their concepts or expressed 'content'. In these instances, the 'hierarchy' that governs 'unification of attitudes', in Brooks' formula, has scant regard for the *form* this thesis or allusion has taken in the parent work. In this, Swift can be praised or blamed. E. P. Thompson, the distinguished marxist historian, uses Swift as his hero to blacken Walpole's name. The 'ascendant Hanoverian Whigs' developed in the 1720s and 1730s 'a sort of State banditry'. Consequently, those Tories who opposed them were on the side of the angels. *Gulliver* can therefore emerge as possessing 'accurate and morally poised comment'.[2] Perry Anderson's objection to this lionising of Swift is perfectly credible. Walpole's most tyrannous penal legislation was most leniently enforced and he did usher in a large measure of religious toleration.[3] His conclusion might redress the balance of history but it does little to illuminate one's reading of the texts.

> In general, intellectual or moral poise—a sense of balance or proportion—is the last quality Swift possessed ... the savagery of Swift's satire, purporting to expose cruelty and inhumanity, compulsively partakes of it—the impulse to brutalize is the perpetual, chill shadow of the design to scandalize .... Foiled ambition and thwarted feeling—Swift's radical blockage in public and private life—are the emotional fires that light the fury of his prose.[4]

This constipated Swift, Anderson borrows from Leavis, who is quoted with approval (pp. 96-9). Both Thompson and Anderson base their aesthetic judgements on Swift's character, the hero/villain who enters the polemical light of day or who regularly reveals his psyche in his rhetoric. The author, and one's opinon of him/her, ordains the work. It is not quite clear what streamlined and poised works Anderson would prefer to Swift's 'radical blockage'. Alignment is not all.

Alternatively, non-alignment is hardly either the condition of the literary critic or the writer. Jacques Derrida's illuminating observation that western language (if not *every* language system) is permeated by a myth of 'presence', a someone who as an individual, utters his/her own individuated perspective, would seem to relegate stands of

131

principle to effects of the will rather than of rational (and therefore linguistic) demonstration. The form of 'textual' criticism this invites can often rest content with conclusions based on how the text displays its purely linguistic fissures or rhetorical flaws. Grant Holly's aim in reading *Gulliver* 'textually' is to analyse how 'Swift's text makes signifying its subject, by implying a vast textuality which incorporates the reader and which, therefore, he can participate in but is no longer free to comment on.' Just in case we took signifying as the signified content of the work, Holly proceeds to show how the 'problematic of differencing along with signifying plays without fear of falling into [a final objective] sense or significance' (p. 135). To put it another way, *Gulliver* cannot represent some imitated reality prior to the form of the text. What occurs is that 'the signified grows out of the signifier.... From this point of view, the text loses its purposiveness and progresses by means of associations which in themselves indicate a compulsive signifying' (p. 151). However, as was pointed out in Chapter 3, such an observation, whilst it may be immensely suggestive, is hardly comprehensive. Just as Thompson and Anderson found the text served one's judgements on Swift, Holly finds history (meaning the author, his ideology and his class) totally inscribed within the text.

In striving to find a middle way between these two pervasive and attractive positions, my aim is to suggest that indeterminacy of meaning need not entail the negation of all historical judgement or explanation. Swift's works are a particularly marked instance of what Robert Martin Adams called (in 1958) 'open form', where their 'literary form ... includes a major unresolved conflict with the intent of displaying its unresolvedness'.[5] Instead of worrying over whether Swift *intended* such ambivalence or not, we ought to attend to the specific historical pressures that help produce Swift's own form of 'logocentrism'. Without such detail, most deconstructive readings resemble a string of footnotes to Derrida or Lacan, but, with this detail, the acknowledgement of the varied authorial functions provide limits to meaning, a significance no longer defined solely within the orbit of a single author's life.

For Swift, the prospect of a mankind constantly remaking norms of conduct in the light of altered historical circumstances and of being Hobbesian 'matter in motion', was not only disturbing but also immensely productive. Gulliver constantly the prey of his experiences when he travels 'into several Remote Nations', the Teller finding truth *and* 'the Integrity of [his] Heart' only in 'this Minute [he is] writing' (I: 22) and the Proposer recommending inhumanity as the last hope for an Irish people who are not only criminally exploited but also tragically undeserving: these are symbols that eventually resist the reduction of paraphrase or the stigma of propaganda. In this, Swift's historical circumstances and his reaction to them actually invite textual readings of his work. When the Teller lays down the 'general Maxim' that 'whatever Reader desires to have a thorow Comprehension of an Author's Thoughts, cannot take a better Method, than by putting himself into the Circumstances and Postures of Life, that the Writer was in, upon every important Passage as it flow'd from his Pen', the result of such epistemology is trivial and irrational, requiring the reader to inhabit a garret bed, go hungry, be under the doctor and have an overdraft. Words must remain significant outside their original context otherwise we would be constrained by the constant necessity of 'a Parity and strict Correspondence of Idea's between the Reader and the Author' (I: 26–7). Unlike in the textual approach, however, Swift tried to keep faith with some spiritual essence called Man that transcended the potential chaos of sense perception and the dead hand of tradition.

Swift's works are, therefore, more symbolic than orderly

'satires' in that they resist a reduction to some prior concept or emotional pattern. In this, Swift is enacting in his works the doubts and contradictions that a less exciting writer would have omitted. Edward Said makes the point that any reader of the *Tale* or *Gulliver* has to 'take seriously Swift's discovery that words and objects in the world are not simply interchangeable, since words extend away from objects into an entirely verbal world of their own' (p. 58). The very difficulty we face when attempting to categorise his writings is just one facet of this critical problem. Genres invite traditional assumptions which in turn breed complacent readers. By rarely establishing a consistent scheme of references to the world of public ritual, even of Christianity, Swift's texts are both imperative and 'open', didactic and interrogative. In these constant redefinitions, such terms as 'reader' and 'author' are not exempt. When, in the 'Epistle Dedicatory' to 'Prince Posterity' in the *Tale*, the Modern Teller attempts to establish his own credentials as writer and the reason why we should spend time reading him, his authority seems evanescent and ephemeral:

> If I should venture in a windy Day, to affirm to *Your Highness*, that there is a large Cloud near the *Horizon*, in the Form of a *Bear*, another in the *Zenith* with the Head of an *Ass*, a third to the Westward with Claws like a *Dragon*; and *Your Highness* Should in a few Minutes think fit to examine the Truth, 'tis certain, they would all be changed in Figure and Position, new ones would arise, and all we could agree upon would be that Clouds there were, but that I was grossly mistaken in the *Zoography* and *Topography* of them. (I: 21)

Such kaleidoscopic variety was just as much a resource as a problem for Swift, for in reading his array of finely inflected voices, we become aware of habit and convention whilst enjoying the possiblity of a freedom from them.

Notes

1. *The Well Wrought Urn*, p. 207.
2. *Whigs and Hunters: The Origins of the Black Act* (London, 1975), p. 294.
3. Anderson acknowledges that the basis for this view can be found in Douglas Hay's 'Property, Authority and the Criminal Law', in *Albion's Fatal Tree*, ed. Douglas Hay *et al.* (London, 1973), pp. 7–63.
4. *Arguments Within English Marxism* (London, 1980), p. 96. For Anderson's full account, see pp. 69–99.
5. *Strains of Discord* (Ithaca, N.Y., 1958), p. 13. For a more Derridean approach, see Neil Saccamano, 'Authority and Publication: The Works of "Swift"', *The Eighteenth Century*, 25 (1984), 241–62.

Chronology

1667   30 November, Swift born in Dublin.

1673   Starts his education at Kilkenny College. Test Act passed, barring Roman Catholics from public office. (Swift took it to be the cornerstone of the Anglican Church.)

1682   Dublin. 24 April, enters Trinity College.

1685   Death of Charles II; accession of James II.

1686   Graduates with a B A degree, *speciali grata* (by special dispensation).

1688   England invaded by William of Orange (later William III); abdication of James II.

1689   Patronage of Sir William Temple. (November) Swift accompanies Temple from Sheen to Moor Park.

1690   Returns to Ireland on medical advice.

1691   Back at Moor Park at Christmas.

1692   *An Ode to the Athenian Society*, his first published work.

1694   Leaves Temple to take holy orders in Ireland. 25 October, ordained deacon. Bank of England established.

1695   13 January, ordained priest. 28 January, granted the Prebendary of Kilroot.

1696   Rejoins Temple. Starts writing *A Tale of a Tub*.

1697   William Dampier publishes his *A New Voyage Round the World*. (His *A Voyage to New Holland* followed in 1703.)

1698   Resigns Kilroot.

1699   27 January, Temple dies. Swift to London, and then to Ireland as Chaplain to the Earl of Berkeley.

1700   22 March, becomes Vicar of Laracor; and September, Prebend of Dunlavin.

1701   Travels to London. At Swift's entreaty, Hester Johnson ('Stella') and her companion Rebecca Dingley join him in Ireland. *Discourse of the Contests and Dissentions between the Nobles and Commons in Athens and Rome, with the Consequences they had upon both those States* (a pro-Whig tract) published in London. War declared by England, Holland and Austria on France (War of the Spanish Succession).

1702   Friendship with leading Whigs in London. Queen Anne succeeds to the throne on death of William.

1703   Arranges for the publication of *A Tale*.

1704   *A Tale of a Tub* published (with *The Battel of the Book* and *Mechanical Operation of the Spirit*) whilst Swift in Ireland.

1707   Returns to England. Meets Esther Vanhomrigh ('Vanessa') for the first time. Act for Union of England and Scotland (implicitly endorsed Scottish Presbyterians).

1708   Meets prominent Whig propagandists, Addison and Steele, in London. *Bickerstaff Papers* and *An Argument against Abolishing Christianity* published.

1710   Fall of the Whig government. Robert Harley (later Earl of Oxford) heads a Tory administration. September, Swift returns to England and meets him.

Begins writing for the Tory *Examiner* periodical.
Begins the *Journal to Stella*.

1711   March, *Miscellanies in Prose and Verse*. June, finishes association with the *Examiner*. 27 November, *The Conduct of the Allies* published, heavily critical of the previous Whig government's handling of the War of the Spanish Succession.

1712   Chief Tory propagandist. February, publishes *Remarks on the Barrier-Treaty* and *Cadenus and Vanessa*.

1713   War ends with the Treaty of Utrecht. April, Swift becomes Dean of St Patrick's, but back in England in October.

1714   February, *The Publick Spirit of the Whigs* published, The Scriblerians (including Pope and Gay) meet for the first time. 27 July, Harley falls. With succession of George I, Tories out of favour. Swift returns to Ireland, followed by Vanessa. Whig ministry formed under Townshend, Stanhope and Walpole.

1719   *Robinson Crusoe* published.

1720   Publishes *A Proposal for the Universal Use of Irish Manufacture* and begins *Gulliver's Travels*. South Sea Bubble.

1721   Walpole becomes first Lord of the Treasury (Prime Minister).

1723   Vanessa dies.

1724–5 *Drapier's Letters* appear.

1725   Wood's halfpence scheme defeated. *Gulliver* completed.

1726   March, in England; April, interview with Walpole. Arranges for publication of *Gulliver*. Returns to Ireland in August. 28 October, *Gulliver* appears in London.

1727   George II succeeds to the throne. Swift visits England for the last time.

1728   28 January, Stella dies.

1729 October, *Modest Proposal* published.

1731 Intense poetic activity. Begins work on *Verses on the Death of Dr Swift*.

1733 *An Epistle to a Lady* and *On Poetry: A Rapsody* published.

1735 Oversees Faulkner's publication of the first volumes of the *Works*.

1738 Senile decay much advanced. *Polite Conversation*, his last complete work, published.

1742 Declared a lunatic.

1745 19 October, Swift dies.

Select Bibliography

*Those works concerned with the textuality of Swift's writing.

Editions

Davis, Herbert *et al.*, *The Prose Writings of Jonathan Swift*, 14 vols (Oxford: Basil Blackwell, 1939–68). The definitive edition. Vol. I contains *A Tale of a Tub, Battel of the Books, The Mechanical Operation of the Spirit* and *The Contests and Dissentions*. Vol. II: *An Argument Against Abolishing Christianity* and the Partridge papers. Vol. IX: the Irish Tracts, 1720–23. Vol X: *Drapier's Letters*. Vol. XI: *Gulliver's Travels*. Vol. XII: Irish Tracts, 1728–33, including *A Modest Proposal*.

Rogers, Pat, *Jonathan Swift: The Complete Poems* (Harmondsworth: Penguin Books; New Haven, N.Y.: Yale University Press, 1983). Not only the complete canon but also a wealth of annotation, particularly on Swift's topical allusions, plus a biographical glossary of his contemporaries.

140

Turner, Paul, *Gulliver's Travels* (Oxford: Oxford University Press, 1971). Concise and informative introduction. Full text with detailed notes.

Williams, Kathleen, *A Tale of a Tub and other Satires* (London: J. M. Dent; New York: E. P. Dutton, 1975). Contains the contents of the 1704 volume plus (among others) *An Argument* and *A Modest Proposal*.

Period Studies

Black, Jeremy (ed), *Britain in the Age of Walpole* (London: Macmillan, 1984). Black's introduction assesses arguments for and against a stable Britain during Walpole's premiership. See also J. A. Downie's 'Walpole, "the Poet's Foe" ' (the literary opposition to Walpole), and Michael Harris' 'Print and Politics in the Age of Walpole' (for evidence of the rapid growth of printed material and its use as propaganda). The Bibliography is comprehensive and up-to-date.

Copley, Stephen (ed.), *Literature and the Social Order in Eighteenth-Century England* (Beckenham, Kent and Dover, New Hampshire: Croom Helm, 1984). Collection of primary sources under several sub-headings. See especially 'Commerce and Industry' for a trading context for *Gulliver* and 'The Poor', views on the conditions of paupers for the Irish tracts.

Harth, Philip, *Swift and Anglican Rationalism: The Religious Background of 'A Tale of a Tub'* (Chicago: University of Chicago Press, 1961). Concentrates just on the religious satire. Pages 101-53 illustrate Swift's distrust of Enthusiasm.

Jacob, Margaret C., *The Newtonians and the English Revolution, 1689-1720* (Hassocks, Sussex; Harvester Press; Ithaca, N.Y.: Cornell University Press, 1976). Science and Free-Thinking. Its impact on the Church is discussed at pp. 72-99 and 201-50.

Lock, F. P., *Swift's Tory Politics* (London: Duckworth, 1983).

Very detailed on Swift's opinion of the Revolution Settlement. His political values expressed in *Gulliver* are considered at pp. 168-79.

Porter, Roy, *English Society in the Eighteenth Century* (Harmondsworth: Penguin Books; New York: Penguin Books, 1982). A general review. The chapter on 'Power, Politics, and the Law' (pp. 113-58) concludes that the propertied classes were unduly favoured by the legal and political system.

Probyn, Clive (ed.), *Jonathan Swift: The Contemporary Background*, (Manchester: Manchester University Press, 1978b). Invaluable primary source material linked by clear explanation and introductions. The sections on 'Ancients and Moderns' and 'The Nature of Man' bear directly on this study.

Rivers, Isabel (ed.), *Books and their Readers in Eighteenth-Century England* (Leicester: Leicester University Press, 1982). Essays on the assumptions writers made, or were entitled to make, about their audiences. See the essays by Terry Belanger (publishers and writers) and W. A. Speck (subscription lists).

Rogers, Pat, *Grub Street: Studies in a Subculture* (London: Methuen, 1972). How the hacks lived: pp. 218-75 deal with *A Tale*. (Reissued as *Hacks and Dunces: Pope, Swift and Grub Street*, 1980).

General Studies

Beaumont, Charles Allen, *Swift's Classical Rhetoric*, University of Georgia Monographs, No. 8 (Athens, Ga: University of Georgia Press, 1961). Swift as rhetorician, especially in his use of the classical essay form. Analysis of *A Modest Proposal* and *An Argument*.

Bullitt, John M., *Jonathan Swift and the Anatomy of Satire: A Study of Satiric Technique* (Cambridge, Mass.: Harvard University Press, 1953). Isolates, New Critically, Swift's rhetorical devices, in order to make large claims for literary satire as a genre.

*Donoghue, Denis, *Jonathan Swift: A Critical Introduction* (Cambridge: Cambridge University Press, 1969). Starts from the premise that the persona is never a reliable narrator in Swift's writing, and that questions of intention are beside the point.

Downie, J. A., *Jonathan Swift: Political Writer* (London: Routledge & Kegan Paul, 1984). A critical biography. More concise and straightforward than Ehrenpreis's work. Valuable and comprehensive chapters on individual texts.

Ehrenpreis, Irvin, *Swift: The Man, His Works, and the Age*, 3 vols. (London: Methuen; Cambridge: Harvard University Press, 1962–83). Exhaustively documented. Vol. 1: *Mr. Swift and his Contemporaries* (1962) (1704 volume). Vol. 2: *Dr. Swift* (1967) (mainly the political writings up to 1714). Vol. 3: *Dean Swift* (1983).

—*Literary Meaning and Augustan Values*, Charlottesville: University Press of Virginia, 1974). Discussed on pp. 42–3

Elliott, Robert, *The Literary Persona* (Chicago: University of Chicago Press, 1982). Attempts to pick holes in both biographical and New Criticism, the one for its naivety, the other for its denigration of the personal element in writing. Pages 107–23 sum up the objections to Ehrenpreis' view of Swift.

Ewald, William, Jr, *The Masks of Jonathan Swift* (Cambridge Mass.: Harvard University Press 1954). Persona criticism (with a vengeance); ignores any historical context at all.

Leavis, F. R., *The Common Pursuit* (London: Chatto & Windus, 1952). Contains 'The Irony of Swift' (pp. 73–87). Famous for its distrust of Swift's 'purely destructive' intensity (p. 75).

*Louis, Frances Deutsch, *Swift's Anatomy of Misunderstanding: A Study of Swift's Epistemological Imagination in A Tale of A Tub and Gulliver's Travels* (London: George Prior Publishers, 1981). Describes how Swift confronted certain contemporary epistemological hypotheses (how we learn about life and ourselves) and highlighted the confusions man inherited.

Manlove, C. N., *Literature and Reality, 1600–1800* (London: Macmillan, 1978). 'The skill of Swift's satire lies in his ability to transmit to us the energy to rebuild even as he demolishes' (p. 114). Sections on *An Argument* and *A Modest Proposal*.

Martz, Louis, L. and Aubrey Williams (eds), *The Author in his Work: Essays on a Problem in Criticism* (New Haven, N.Y.: Yale University Press, 1978). See David Vieth's 'The Mystery of Personal Identity: Swift's Verses on His Own Death' (pp. 245–62). Treats the poem as a hoax, calculated to 'transform the image of Jonathan Swift into a teleological fulfillment of history' (p. 258) whereby his self-image is the real subject of the poem.

Nokes, David, *Jonathan Swift, A Hypocrite Reversed: A Critical Biography* (Oxford: Oxford University Press, 1985). More a biography than a string of critical readings, but an accessible and lucid account of the major Works. *A Tale* is discussed at pp. 43–52 and *Gulliver* pp. 317–29.

Price, Martin, *Swift's Rhetorical Art: A Study in Structure and Meaning* (New Haven, N.Y.: Yale University Press, 1953; rpt. Hamden, Conn.: Archon Books, 1963; Carbondale, Ill.: Southern Illinois University Press, 1973). Attempts to isolate Swift's most typical patterns of expression.

—*To the Palace of Wisdom: Studies in Order and Energy from Dryden to Blake* (Carbondale, Ill.: Southern Illinois Unversity Press; London: Feffer & Simons Inc., 1964). Stresses the disorder of much Augustan writing. Extended readings of *Gulliver* (pp. 198–204) and *A Tale* (pp. 208–16).

Probyn, Clive (ed.), *The Art of Jonathan Swift* (New York: Barnes & Noble; London: Vision Press, 1978a). A varied collection of essays. David Nokes' '"Hack at Tom Poley's": Swift's Use of Puns' (pp. 43–56) dwells on Swift's delight in non-mimetic word-play.

*Rawson, Claude, *Gulliver and the Gentle Reader: Studies in Swift and our Time* (London: Routledge & Kegan Paul,

1973). Not just on *Gulliver*. Swift's tactic of attacking the reader's habitual assumptions is seen to implicate the author too. Provocative.

—(ed.), *The Character of Swift's Satire: A Revised Focus* (Newark, Del.: University of Delaware Press; London: Associated University Press, 1983). A revised edition of Rawson's essay, 'The Character of Swift's Satire' (pp. 21–82) is stimulating in its description of Swift's conflict between instinctual sin and redemptive traditions. John Traugott's 'A Tale of a Tub' (pp. 83–126) holds out sympathy for Swift's vividly evil character sketches.

Said, Edward W., *The World, the Text, and the Critic* (Cambridge, Mass., Harvard University Press; London: Faber & Faber, 1984). In two provoking essays, 'Swift's Tory Anarchy' (pp. 54–71) and 'Swift as Intellectual' (pp-72–89), Said describes the 'worldly' (that is, not *totally* textual) nature of Swift's writing.

Steele, Peter, *Jonathan Swift: Preacher and Jester* (Oxford: Clarendon Press, 1978). As with many recent 'mimetic' studies, the accommodation of the contradictory elements of play and rule is engaging, even if the conclusions are safe and familiar.

*Zimmerman, Everett, *Swift's Narrative Satires: Author and Authority*, (Ithaca, N.Y.: Cornell University Press, 1983). Concentrates on *A Tale* and *Gulliver*. 'Instead of allowing the reader to assume the existence of an authoritative author from whom the satire emanates, Swift requires the reader to search for the principle of authority that validates the satire' (p. 13).

Books and Articles on Particular Works

(a) A Tale of a Tub

*Atkins, G. Douglas, *Reading Deconstruction/Deconstructive Reading*, (Lexington, Ken.: University Press of Kentucky, 1983). An account of Deconstruction's anti-humanism (pp. 15–33) forms a prelude to several readings of

Restoration and Augustan texts. The discussion of *A Tale* (pp. 105–17) follows the American critic Paul de Man in claiming how interchangeable 'blindness and insight' could be in literary and critical matters: 'The supposedly insightful (i.e. satirical) text may then appear most blind in condemning the blind but insightful Hack' (p. 117).

Clark, John R., *Form and Frenzy in Swift's Tale of a Tub* (Ithaca, N.Y.: Cornell University Press, 1970). A 'mimetic' reading, stressing Swift's artistry in creating the most unfamiliar modes of cohesion.

De Porte, Michael V., *Nightmares and Hobby Horses: Swift, Sterne, and Augustan Ideas of Madness* (San Marino, Calif.: Huntingdon, 1974). A study of Augustan theories of mental disorder and their application to Swift's 'psychology' in *A Tale* (especially pp. 60–89).

*Kenner, Hugh, *The Stoic Comedians* (London: W. H. Allen, 1964). Regards *A Tale* as a product of the rapid recognition that the world of print entailed different writing (and reading) techniques. The section directly concerned with *A Tale* is at pp. 37–42.

*Korkowski, Eugene, 'With an Eye to the Bunghole: Figures of Containment in *A Tale of a Tub*', *Studies in English Literature*, 15 (1975), 391–408. Swift's tub stands for all types of containment, inaugurating a major area of rhetorical play between the Teller's and our preconceptions as to what is inside/outside, relevant/irrelevant and real/false.

Rogers, Pat, 'Form in *A Tale of a Tub*', *Essays In Criticism*, 22 (1972), 142–60. Finds the real flaw of the work in too much form (to the point of redundancy) rather than formlessness.

*Smith, Frederik N., *Language and Reality in Swift's A Tale of a Tub*, (Columbus, Ohio: Ohio State University Press, 1979). Argues that it is *style* that creates meaning in *A Tale* and places Swift's satire in a linguistic context. Valuable research and conclusions.

(b) *Gulliver's Travels*

*Castle, Terry J., 'Why the Houynhnms Don't Write: Swift, Satire and the Fear of the Text', *Essays in Literature* (Western Illinois University), 7 (1980), 31–44. Traces Swift's perception through *Gulliver* and *A Tale* that there is a fearful gap between speech and writing and that one of the Houynhnm community's greatest virtues could be a lack of writing.

Davis, Lennard J., *Factual Fictions: The Origins of the English Novel* (New York: Columbia University Press, 1983). Explores the paradox of the 'factual fiction' and how the novel only became possible with the new criteria of truth and recentness fostered by journalistic discourses. Not directly on *Gulliver*, but the chapters 'Theories of Fiction in Early English Novels' (pp. 102–22) and 'The Language Of Print' (pp. 138–53) are indispensable.

*Holly, Grant, 'Travel and Translation: Textuality in *Gulliver's Travels*', *Criticism*, 21 (1979), 134–52. Attempts to show how the process of signifying is the true subject of *Gulliver*.

*Keener, Frederick M., *The Chain of Becoming: The Philiosophical Tale, The Novel, and a Neglected Realism of the Enlightenment: Swift, Montesquieu, Voltaire, Johnson and Austen* (New York: Columbia University Press, 1983). Treats the philosophical tale as a serious art form. The chapter on Gulliver (pp. 89–126) constructs a convincing argument that the contemporary genres Swift satirises— almanac, project and traveller's tale—help determine Gulliver's mind through the conventions of print and a Lockean association of ideas.

*Kelly, Ann Cline, 'After Eden: Gulliver's (Linguistic) Travels', *Journal of English Literary History*, 45 (1978), 33–54. Swift regarded as a satirist of those rationalising ('Edenic') linguists who fail to recognise that man is a fallen creature.

Lock, F. P., *The Politics of Gulliver's Travels* (Oxford: Clarendon Press, 1980). Directs the reader's attention to Swift's general targets rather than the personal and

147

particular allusions of footnotes.

Reiss, Timothy, *The Discourse of Modernism* (New Haven, N.Y.: Yale University Press, 1983). Starts from the observation that the 'analytic-referential' discourse of experimentalism is one that Swift distrusted and one that the Houynhnms manifested. A particular type of *rhetoric* provides Swift's contemporaries' notions of truth, not *reality*. In the chapter on *Gulliver* (pp. 328–50), Reiss attempts to show how Swift questions its dominance and therefore the Houynhnms too.

(c) *The Irish Tracts*

Ferguson, Oliver, *Jonathan Swift and Ireland* (Urbana, Ill.: University of Illinois Press, 1962). The most complete and authoritative account of Swift's Irish years. Champions Swift as an Irish patriot.

Hilson, J. C., M.M.B. Jones and J. R. Watson (eds.), *Augustan Worlds: New Essays in Eighteenth-Century Literature* (New York: Barnes & Noble; Leicester: Leicester University Press, 1978). See Claude Rawson's 'A Reading of A Modest Proposal' (pp. 29–50), where he takes the Proposer's comments on the poor as a burden to the country as unironic. Reprinted in Rawson's *Order from Confusion Sprung: Studies in Eighteenth-Century Literature from Swift to Cowper*, 1985, pp. 121–44.

Nokes, David, 'Swift and the Beggars', *Essays in Criticism*, 26 (1976), 218–35. Draws on Swift's sermons to show that he could regard economic ills as man's lot. In his satire, however, he could still arraign the government for the condition of the poor.

Rawson, Claude, 'The Injured Lady and the Drapier: A Reading of Swift's Irish Tracts', *Prose Studies*, 3 (1980), 15–43. An account of how the Drapier could be merely a rhetorical voice, calculated to be penetrated through to a 'very evident presence' and whose 'self-projections' are rescued thereby from too much self-revelation (pp. 30–1).

Index

Locke, John, 33, 69–71, 93,
95, 105, 143
- *Essay Concerning Human
Understanding*, 26, 51,
69–71
- *The Reasonableness of
Christianity*, 18
Louis, Frances, 54, 139–40

Madden, Dr Samuel, 96–7
Man, Paul de, 142
Mandeville, Bernard de, 23–4,
28
Manlove, C. N., 29, 120, 140
Martz, Louis, 140
McCormack, W. J., 94
Memoirs of Martinus Scriblerus,
83
Midleton, Lord Chancellor,
115
Milton, John, 12
Molesworth, Viscount, 115,
117
Molyneux, William, 125
Montagu, Charles, 76
Montaigne, Michel de, 52–3
Motte, Benjamin, 57–8

Navigation Acts (1663, 1666),
99, 118
New Critics 2–5, 43–5, 118–
19, 120, 129–30, 138–9
Nokes, David, 23, 27, 128,
140, 144
Nonconformity, 10, 14, 15,
18–19, 65

Occasional Conformity, 19
Oldmixon, John, 26–7

Parks, George, B., 94

Partridge, John, 10–13, 19–20,
33, 40, 47
Patey, Douglas Lane, 95
Paulson, Ronald, 43, 44
Petty, Sir William, 105
Pope, Alexander, 13, 60, 74,
80, 97, 98
- *The Dunciad*, 13
- *Epistle to Bathurst*, 102–3
- *Essay on Man*, 86–7
Porter, Roy, 138
Poyning's Law (1494), 99,
114, 118
Presbyterians, 18, 30
*Present Miserable State of
Ireland, The* 96–7, 103
Price, Martin, 5, 23–4, 68,
118, 119, 140
Prior, Matthew, 92
Probyn, Clive, 138, 140

Quintana, Ricardo, 4

Rawson, Claude, 52–3, 74,
111–12, 126, 128, 140–1,
144
Reiss, Timothy, 79, 144
Rivers, Isabel, 138
Rochefoucauld, François, duc
de la, 95
Rogers, Pat, 13, 93, 136, 138,
142
Ross, Angus, 58, 93
Rousseau, Jean-Jacques, 76
Royal Society, 76, 79–81, 90,
93

Saccamano, Neil, 135
Said, Edward, 8, 91, 134, 141
Scaliger, Julius, 36
Scarborough, Lord, 93

MLib